WHY DEVELOP YOUR PSYCHIC POWERS?

Because they are a natural, and fundamental, part of you: without them, you lack certain abilities that contribute to your success and fulfillment in life.

The program of development described in this book is both enjoyable and practical. Following it, you will gain in health and vitality, emotional and mental strength, greater success in your daily pursuits, and a new understanding of your Inner Self and the World in which we all live.

You will learn techniques of relaxation and restoration for the Body, Psyche and Mind. You will also learn two special meditation programs: the *Tabor Formulation* and the *Reflection on the Psycho-physical Unity,* and you will learn the value of new attitudes to all the things you do—including *Imaginative Enthusiasm,* the secret to a happy and well-balanced life.

In developing your psychic powers—those of ESP, Telekinesis, Astral Vision, Divination, Psychometry, Dowsing, etc.—you will open new doors to knowledge and adventure that will enrich your life in all dimensions.

And in developing your own psychic powers, and in understanding the description of the psyche given in this book, you will gain new insight into the natural development of the child and immensely improve your ability as a parent or teacher to help children grow into more complete human beings.

Fun! Many of the "exercises" in this development program are GAMES that can be played by all ages for enjoyment as well as the growth of the skills involved.

Why develop your Psychic Powers? *Because you are missing out on so much without them!*

About the Authors

Melita Denning and Osborne Phillips, the authors of this book and others in this series, are internationally recognized and honored authorities on Occultism, the Western Mystery Tradition, and the psychology of mystical and religious experience.

They are listed in a number of reference works, including *Who's Who in the World* and the *Dictionary of International Biography*. Their profound researches into the religious mysteries and magical practices, and their many years of intense practical involvement in Initiate Orders, amply qualify them to make this once secret knowledge available to the average person.

To Write to the Authors

We cannot guarantee that every letter written to the authors can be answered, but all will be forwarded on to them. Both the authors and the publisher appreciate hearing from readers, learning of your enjoyment and benefit from this book. Llewellyn also publishes a regularly issued tabloid newspaper of news and reviews of practical esoteric studies, and some readers' questions and comments to the authors may be answered through this newspaper's columns if permission to do so is included in the original letter. The authors sometimes participate in seminars and workshops, and dates and places are announced in the *Llewellyn News and Reviews* newspaper. To write to the authors, or to ask a question, or to secure a free copy of this newspaper, write to:

Denning and Phillips
c/o LLEWELLYN PUBLICATIONS
P.O. Box 43383-DPP, St. Paul, MN 55164-0383, U.S.A.
Please enclose a self-addressed, stamped envelope for reply, or $1.00

About The Llewellyn Practical Guides
to Personal Power

PRACTICAL: available, usable, and valuable in actions applied to useful purposes, contributing toward a better life.

That's what we mean when we say these books are "practical." The knowledge is communicated in a manner that makes it immediately available and usable to the reader: it's not speculative or abstract knowledge, nor merely informative or entertaining.

And it is valuable! Here are techniques that will help you to a better life, will help you attain things that you want, will help you in your personal growth and development. More than that, these books can change your life, dynamically, positively.

Success against all obstacles! Miracles of healing! Powers of ESP, psycho-kinesis, out-of-body travel! Clairvoyance and divination of the future! Amazing powers of mind and body! Attainment of all desires! Communication with non-physical beings! Knowledge by non-material means!

We've always known of things like this . . . seemingly supernormal achievements, often by quite ordinary people. Are these things really possible? Can such powers be ours? Can we actually take control of our own lives?

Yes, we know that many things are possible, and yet we so rarely achieve all that we desire. We are told that we use only 10% of our mental capacity, that faith can move mountains, that love heals all hurt. We believe, but we lack practical knowledge.

All things that you will ever want must have their start in your mind. In these books you are given practical knowledge and progressive exercises to develop your inner powers. You are given specific techniques for the application of these powers. These abilities will eventually belong to everybody through natural evolution: you can attain them now through self-directed programs of development and training.

OTHER BOOKS FROM THE AUTHORS

The Magical Philosophy—A Study of the Western Mystery Tradition
>Book I, *Robe and Ring*, 1974
>Book II, *The Apparel of High Magick*, 1975
>Book III, *The Sword and the Serpent*, 1975
>Book IV, *The Triumph of Light*, 1978
>Book V, *Mysteria Magica*, 1982

The Llewellyn Practical Guide(s) to:
>*Astral Projection*, 1979
>*Creative Visualization*, 1980
>*Psychic Self-Defense & Well-Being*, 1980
>*The Development of Psychic Powers*, 1981
>*The Magick of Sex*, 1982
>*The Magick of the Tarot*, 1983

The Llewellyn Mystery Religion series:
>*Voudoun Fire: The Living Reality of Mystical Religion*, 1979

The Llewellyn Deep Mind Tape(s) for:
>*Astral Projection and the Out-of-Body experience*, 1981

Other Books Forthcoming:
>*The Llewellyn Complete Guide to Planetary Magick,*
>*Crowley on Magick,*
>*The Llewellyn Practical Guide to Qabalistic Meditation*
>*The Llewellyn Working Manual to the Formula*
>*of the Magician*

Also Forthcoming:
>*A correspondence Course on the Western Mystery Tradition*

Write for full list of forthcoming titles
and current information on related publications.

LLEWELLYN PUBLICATIONS
P.O. Box 43383-DPP, St. Paul, MN 55164-0383, U.S.A.

The Llewellyn Practical Guide to

The Development of
Psychic Powers

by Melita Denning and Osborne Phillips

1983
Llewellyn Publications
St. Paul, Minnesota, 55164, 0383, U.S.A.

International Standard Book Number: 0-87542-191-1
Library of Congress Catalog Card Number:
First Edition 1981
First Printing 1981
Second Printing 1982
Third Printing 1983
Production by Llewellyn Publications
Publication by Llewellyn Publications
Typography & Art property of Chester-Kent, Inc.

LLEWELLYN PUBLICATIONS

A Division of Chester-Kent, Inc.
P.O. Box 43383
St. Paul, MN 55164-0383, U.S.A.

Printed in the United States of America

Illustrations by Joanne Westbrook

1983
Llewellyn Publications
St. Paul, Minnesota 55164-0383, U.S.A.

Introduction

Psychic Powers!

Who has not dreamed of possessing amazing powers —powers to move objects without physically touching them, to see at a distance or into the future, to know the thoughts of another person, to read the past of an object or person, to find water or mineral wealth by dowsing—and more?

But, most people have been taught to either think such abilities to be mere fantasies—really dreams!—or else as the special gift of a limited few, or of those who are blessed with special religious grace.

This book says that psychic abilities are natural to everyone! They are not merely fantasy, but real and a dynamic part of your total mind/body/soul/spirit whole being that should not be neglected. These powers are not limited to especially religious people, and certainly are not limited to any one religious affiliation—although it may be true that the style of life, the dietary and excercise habits, the meditations, and the love of nature and life that often is part of a personal religious way, are indeed conducive to the development of these powers.

Further, this book says that the unusual psychic abilities of a few people are no more a special gift that is theirs exclusively than is unusual athletic or musical or artistic ability. True—if we do not have an unusual heritage giving us perhaps a wonderfully healthy and strong body, no amount of training and exercise is likely to turn us into Olympic champions; but it is also true that anyone who is not crippled or handicapped can develop more than average athletic prowess, if that person follows a sensible life-style in pursuit of that goal. Great dancers, for instance, are not born—their greatness is achieved by following a program of development.

Yes, some people are born with a greater natural inclination or a greater natural talent in a certain direction—but all of us can develop any or many of the entire range of powers and abilities that have ever been part of the human heritage.

This is especially true of psychic abilities—for they are not only natural to us, they have their source in the instinctive-emotional level of the psyche that is the oldest and most fundamental part of our evolutionary heritage.

We don't usually experience these psychic powers because our modern life-style has repressed their natural development. But, they are there, and even repressed they sometimes manifest in moments of need, or personal crisis, or because of trauma or unusual external stimulus. Sometimes, in some instances, they manifest because of an example that seems to start a kind of contagion: even people who witness psychic demonstrations sometimes start to spontaneously produce the same phenomena.

We live in glorious times! We have extended the capacity of technology to bring us one wonderful benefit after another—computers replace and far exceed the capacity of the calculators that replaced the adding machines of just 50 years ago; we now travel regularly at speeds matching, even exceeding, the speed of sound; music can be electronically synthesized, reproduced and broadcast—and the equipment reduced from weighty pieces of furniture to miniatures that can be carried on a person; word processors have built-in memories with 50,000 word vocabularies that can correct our spelling and even translate from one language into another; we can cut through thick steel at fast speeds with a laser beam; travel to the moon; or . . . blast a city into nothing, and threaten to destroy all life on this one beautiful planet!

In just a dozen years we have seen the previously thought limits in nearly every technical field far surpassed—and we now know that we will be able to continually extend the capacity of our machines and devices.

But—what have we done with our capacity as human beings? We know that we function far below our potential: it is those exceptions to the norm that prove this, and that give us some glimpse of the extent of our heritage. What any human can do, or has done, we all could do. And, whatever has been achieved in the past can be exceeded in the future.

So, why don't we do more?

Our limitations—as humans—are self-imposed; as individuals, however, we suffer for the sins of our parents and teachers and other authorities who taught us what could not be done. And now we see that these limits can be undone, and this book shows us that the method is simple: start playing games! (Become as little children?) All growth is joy; all achievement is adventure; and the expression of our "wholeness" is ecstasy!

* * *

Please read this book completely through so as to gain an overall view of the ground covered, and of the general plan of development, before you undertake a program of development. It doesn't matter, really, what you start with—ESP cards, scrying, dowsing, etc.—but it is a good idea to work some with all these abilities.

Remember—your psychic powers are a natural part of your life as a human being. You are not trying to graft anything on from the outside; you are not like a horse pulling a cart, but more like a bird learning to fly: it's a natural expression of your growth into a more whole person. So be happy about it, like the flying birds! Psychic development is play and fun, so enjoy! This book tells you how.

We have not described every kind of psychic power in this book — there are some, like "Astral Projection," that require detailed treatment in individual Llewellyn Practical Guides. What we have done in this book is to include explicit details on developing some important and topical psychic abilities, with two important meditation techniques that will aid your general psychic unfoldment.

The Tabor Formulation that is given in Chapter One will slowly and safely enhance your mental and psychic powers, give you physical and emotional renewal, and bring you into active participation with the spiritual reality filling the Universe.

The Reflection on the Psycho-physical Unity that is given in Chapter Three will strengthen the interaction of all levels of the psyche and the Higher

Self, and prevent any imbalance that would interfere with your becoming more receptive and aware of inspiration and guidance from the Divine Source. It will bring about the integration of all levels in their greater strength and development to make you a more powerful, a more whole, person.

Perhaps the most exciting aspect of psychic development is the new relationship you will discover to the World around you: your increased range of awareness will extend to other dimensions than you have sensed before, you will perceive subtle vibrations in familiar things that you overlooked before, you will find new richness in other people, and the lives of children will take on even greater beauty. You will never again see a dull landscape: Nature will open new doors to your extended sensibilities. The Universe itself will beckon you: you will never again be confined to one small private world.

* * *

One short, final note. We, the authors and the publisher, do like to hear from readers. We especially like to know of your progress, the results of your own researches, the successes you will have. The authors can't answer every letter, of course—but if you do look for a reply, please include a stamped and self-addressed envelope. And if you are asking a question, please be as concise and direct as possible, and allow space for an answer right on your letter.

If you do start a group for psychic adventure and mutual growth, tell us about that too, and perhaps a time will come when we can help with relating the work of one group to that of another—long distance experiments, for example. We would like, occasionally, to be able to report on the activities of your group, or your own successes, in our newsletter: so, if you write something that we might be able to publish, give us enough details, and be sure to say that we're free to publish your report. And if you are not on our mailing list, drop a note to our Customer Service Dept. and ask to be placed on it. That way you will learn of some of these activities, and any new developments.

And, finally, I want to wish you much luck and enjoyment in your new venture into the development of your psychic powers!

Carl Llewellyn Weschke
Publisher

Contents

Llewellyn Record Sheets

"Study Points" are part of the unique approach used in the Llewellyn Practical Guides series of books dealing with the 'technology' of Magick and the seemingly super-normal powers of the Deep Mind. "Study Points" outline certain concepts important to the chapter that follows—not as an outline of the contents, but as points which are emphasized by calling them to your attention in advance of the context in which they will appear.

Each chapter is followed by a "Check Point" which serves as re-inforcement of certain of the concepts, and of the practices, that have been presented. The "Check Point" is more than a review; it is a reiteration of the steps taken in the steady and progressive development in this practical and modern method of training the hidden faculties of mind and psyche.

Study Points

1

1. Psychic Powers are part of your *rightful* heritage, and their development will bring you enjoyment and satisfaction, as well as many practical and spiritual benefits.

2. Your Psyche and your body make up a very closely-united whole—neither the one nor the other acts quite alone, and both work better when we recognize their basic interaction.

   a. "Psychic Power" generally means the assertion of the psyche's powers in the material world without the apparent involvement of the physical body.

   b. But, "Psychic Power" is also involved when the physical body exceeds the usual level of strength or skill—as in athletic or sports achievements, dance, or feats of strength. In other words, the

development of the psyche can also directly benefit the body.

3. "Games" involve the interaction of psyche and body,
    and the Mental Attitude of "game-playing" con-
    tributes to the manifestation of your psychic powers,
    and to their further development.
    a. This mental attitude can be described as one of
       enthusiasm, total absorption, thoroughness, "liv-
       ing-the-part," "making-believe," etc.
    b. The testing of psychic skills should involve a
       game-setting creating "imaginative enthusiasm"
       among the participants.

4. Because of the interaction of psyche and body, your
    interest in the development of your psychic powers
    also means that you should concern yourself with the
    health and well-being of your physical body.
    a. A diet that includes fresh and raw fruits and
       vegetables will be beneficial.
    b. Aerobic exercises increase the oxygen available
       to the body, and should be done strenuously
       enough to raise the heartbeat to about 140 per
       minute for several minutes.
    c. Rest is also vital. In addition to proper sleep, the
       process of "meditation" taught in this book can
       be called "an exercise in relaxation," and is help-
       ful in resting the brain and nerves. Daily meditation
       is part of your development program.

5. "The Tabor Formulation" meditation should be performed at least once daily, and always to precede any psychic practices.

   Rules for the Tabor Formulation:
   a. Sit comfortably, quite still, palms on thighs.
   b. Stage One—Breathing:
   Lower gaze, fixing it upon your navel.
   Breath in an even, gentle manner, deeply but without strain.
   Your attention is occupied entirely with your breathing.
   c. Stage Two—Light:
   On an in-breath, become aware of a nebulous radiation of golden light from just below your breastbone, forming a luminous cloud halfway between your navel and your chin.
   Be aware of this Light as Love, and keep your attention occupied entirely with this Light and with your breathing.
   d. Stage Three—Silent Utterance:
   Retain awareness of breathing and of the Light. Silently "utter" mantrams in your mind, one on an in-breath, another on the out-breath.
      Choose words or phrases that affirm your Oneness with the Cosmos—giving and receiving Light and Life, and transmuting that which you breathe in into that which you breathe out. This is the heart of the meditation.

6. List of equipment you will need (instructions for making your own are in the text):
   a. Pendulum, preferably of wood.
   b. ESP cards.
   c. Vision Mirror.
   d. Log book.

1

Inspiration and

Equipment

You have a body, and you also have a psyche. You probably have a fair idea of the powers of your body, or of body and psyche together; now you want to find out how to exercise your psyche's powers specifically.

As a fact, body and psyche together make up a very closely-united whole, and to expect either one or the other to act quite alone would be unrealistic. Still, what we mean by the use of psychic power is a very well defined form of activity. For example: if you wish to lift a pencil off the table, and you merely sit looking at it until it trembles, tilts, and at last rises up above the table, that is a demonstration of psychic power even though your physical energy undoubtedly helps. But if you grasp the pencil and lift it by hand, of course you show no special power even though your psyche most certainly is what causes your muscles to act.

5

At the same time, it is becoming better recognized nowadays that even in activities which are classified as physical, such as athletics or dancing, the higher levels of skill really involve considerable psychic action, whether the athletes or dancers themselves are aware of this or not.

Such a simple series of movements as bending down and touching your toes can convince you of the importance of the psyche's action in bodily movement. Most people can touch their toes, even if it causes a slight discomfort in the backs of the legs and thighs; they simply reach their hands up overhead as high as possible and then bring them down, bending at shoulders and hips together. If you can normally do this, or get fairly close, try it and test how it feels.

Next, however, try to do the same thing in the manner of someone who doesn't really expect success or who is nervous of trying. The doubters raise their arms, then gently bend over the top part of the spine, and then the waist, and so get into a position from which, as a fact, it's *impossible* to bend down and touch the toes, try as they will.

That shows what the non-material part of you, the psyche, can do for your bodily organism by its mere expectation of success or of failure. *And that's only a very crude, obvious example.*

Now you are going to train and develop your real psychic abilities, but first we are going to test what you have to begin with. You may be surprised!

This gives you an early opportunity, too, to get some of your friends interested in your projects. That way, you'll have people who can give you important help in the various tests and practices, who can bring an element of companionship and of good-natured competition into what you are doing. That way, also, you'll avoid scaring your friends as you might if you began suddenly demonstrating strange skills later on. If they are in at the start, and above all if they try some of the experiments for themselves, they'll not find it too startling or odd later on when you—and they—can do far more than at present.

Don't be too serious when you invite your friends to join you. You are going to try some *games.* THAT'S THE BEST MENTAL ATTITUDE FOR SUCCESS. Most people understand the right kind of seriousness to give to a "game" — naturally they try to win but they don't attach life-and-death importance to it, and they allow their imagination and their sense of pleasure some real place in the action.

You see this in games of chance, so-called: in a casino. (Maybe one day there will be no more "games of chance" because people will understand the natural laws which govern them; but at this present time, there's still "chance.") You may know the type of the successful gambler: sometimes he (or she) loses and doesn't take it too much to heart, but puts immense enthusiasm into winning; and it's *imaginative enthusiasm,* with almost the vivid zest of a child's play-world.

Next, so as to understand this better, we can take a quick look at the animal world. Young living creatures of every kind work very hard at developing their various abilities, whatever special powers they will need in order to live effectively the kind of life which is to be theirs: running swiftly, or stalking, leaping or climbing or swimming, biting or butting. We see whatever actions are most essential to the life of that creature acted out, over and over, in the play of the young ones. Play? Of course it's play, the most carefree and wholehearted play imaginable; but it's play with a serious purpose, however unconsciously.

Human children do this too, up to a point. Just as we know that before birth the developing infant grows through the principal stages of human evolution, so, from birth onwards, we find the child's brain and physical abilities developing through the various stages of human progress: walking upright, talking, holding, riding, building, shaping clay, drawing, making purposed sounds for pleasure, and so on. Too, we see children acting out in play whatever situations they see to be important in adult life: weddings and funerals, shopping, going on vacation, family life. Usually they go on playing at these games until they have, as far as they can at that time, *"assimilated"* the skill or the situation, come to terms with its physical or emotional content. Sometimes, as frequently happens in games having a sexual connotation, someone stops the children before they find out "too much."

But there are other games a lot of children play, games based on stories of wonder, miracles, magick or science fiction or straight out of the children's own imagination — visualized playmates, animated toys, historical or legendary characters — and often people have described how in their childhood the "make-believe" of such games gradually became real. Meaningful messages were given by an imagined being, real telepathy or telekinesis took place, wishes "came true," and the young players found an objective reality in their own psychic powers.

Unfortunately such discoveries also, if older folk hear of them, are usually stopped or brushed aside as "only imagination," or "romancing," or "you're too big for that kind of thing now," or "Tommy must have been playing some kind of trick." (Funny thing is, Tommy or Daisy very often *was* playing some kind of trick — at first! It was a game, but soon it really worked!)

So whether the faculties we want to develop are of the body or of the psyche, the best way to set about it is in the spirit of a game: a game played in earnest, but not in *grim* earnest. Think yourself into the right attitude for psychic development: don't just try to "act the part," you need really to live it. Call to mind all the fun you would have had if you'd always had these powers developed: think of the enhanced joy in living, *the endless interest and deep pleasure you are going to have now,* the satisfaction of developing the faculties which are your rightful heritage.

Taste that interest, pleasure and satisfaction *now*. Recall within yourself the enthusiasm, the total absorption, the thoroughness which go into children's games; you need to give those qualities to developing your psychic faculties. You owe it to yourself, because here's a part of yourself which got left out when you were attending to your athletics, your studies, your hobbies, all the activities you grew up with.

So you are one united person: your body and psyche are accustomed to working together, and work best in that way. Because of this, you would do well, both as a preliminary and as an accompaniment to your psychic development program, to make sure your body is as fit and as energetic as you can reasonably have it.

If you are in normally good health to begin with, there are three main factors to take into consideration so you'll stay that way, and hopefully improve your general condition beyond your expectations. They are *diet, rest,* and *exercise.*

With regard to diet, if you have no specific individual problems, you would do well to study some of the up-to-date findings on the subject. We give some guidelines in other books in this series: there exist also a number of books on holistic health by various authors, many of which give sane, practical advice on healthy eating. Find out what is best for you; but in any event, *let a good proportion of your food be raw,* as in salads, granola, fresh fruit, muesli etc.

It's important that you get enough *rest*. The amount of *sleep* which is good for a person varies from one to another, but for anyone in normal health seven or eight hours should suffice. Too much sleep can cause drowsiness and a craving for yet more sleep. If you sleep well and still feel drowsy in the mornings, try a brisk walk. First thing in the morning or just after lunch, walking can usually dispel sleepy feelings by speeding up the circulation and putting more oxygen into the blood. If you still have a problem, you can need either a negative ionizer or a doctor's advice; but even with no problem you can need more *rest*, which is by no means the same thing as sleep.

Basically, when you are not actively using your body you should relax it and rest it; and whenever you are not actively using your brain, you should try to stop using it for a time as far as you can. Your *mind*, strictly, doesn't need rest; but, unless you monitor some of its activities, it can tire out your brain and nervous systems needlessly and uselessly.

You can rest your brain and nerves by *meditation.*

The form of meditation we recommend for use in the development of psychic powers is based on an early medieval Western mystical technique. YOU SHOULD BRING IT TO FULL PROFICIENCY BEFORE START-ING ON ANY OTHER PRACTICES IN THIS BOOK. *When you have fully developed it, you should use it to precede all psychic practices.*

This meditation should be performed at least once a day, since the release of energy and sense of well-being which it causes are of great benefit in strengthening and intensifying psychic powers.

A group which meets for psychic purposes should open every meeting with this meditation; a group form of it is given in Appendix B, and the same rule applies as for personal use: the *group is to be proficient in the meditation before attempting the other practices in this book.*

Perform your personal meditation always at one same time of day if possible. If however you are going to do psychic practices, whether alone or in group, at another time on a particular day, then, since you will have meditation to precede that, you can *if you wish* omit your regular meditation time on that day.

We call this meditation method:

The Tabor Formulation

All garments worn for this meditation should be loose-fitting; *this should be taken as a general recommendation for all psychic practices.* Sit in a balanced position with the spine vertical. Be easy and natural; there are a few rules which must be observed in this procedure, but they only require very reasonable effort, while the benefits are great.

An important rule, when once you have taken up your position, is *to keep quite still.* Place the palms of your hands on your thighs and keep them there.

Make sure to sit comfortably: if for example you find you need a cushion, then have one next time.

Your body, or rather your Lower Unconscious working through your nervous systems, may try to distract you. This will not necessarily happen, but learners do often find a quite subjective tickle starting up in the nose, or a nerve jumping in the leg, or some peculiar sensation disturbing throat, chest, stomach or so on. *Pay no attention and it will go.*

This meditation is organized in three stages, which are cumulative in content: Stage Two contains the material of Stage One, Stage Three contains the material of Stages One and Two.

STAGE ONE: SIMPLE BREATHING

Lower your gaze, fixing it upon your navel or a point in that region. Breathe in an even, gentle manner as deeply as you can without strain. If your mind wanders, as soon as you notice bring it back gently but firmly to your breathing.

STAGE TWO: AWARENESS OF THE LIGHT

Entering into the second stage of the meditation, *on an in-breath* be aware of a nebulous radiation of golden light, which is also a radiation of love, from just below your sternum; it seems to form a luminous cloud about midway between your navel (at which you continue to gaze down) and your chin.

You don't have to do anything about that light. Simply be aware of it, of being illuminated by it, of being loved by it. Accept that awareness; don't think about it, don't even try to aspire to it. Just keep on being conscious of it, and of your breathing.

Any time your attention strays, bring it back to the light and to your breathing.

STAGE THREE: SILENT UTTERANCE

Retaining awareness of your breathing and of the light, silently "utter" *mantrams* — phrases or single words — which you feel to be suited to your meditation: formulate each word distinctly in your mind, but with no vocalization or movement of the mouth. You will need two mantrams to use together, one for the in-breath and one for the out-breath. Their chief purpose is to express in brief compass something of your essential relationship with the Cosmos. It is to affirm your bond of oneness with the Cosmos: that bond in which you are sustained by the beneficence of the Whole, at the same time participating actively in the Whole. You are a living and purposing component of it, giving forth again with blessing that which you receive.

Examples of suitable mantrams are:

On an in-breath: Light and Life fill me.
On an out-breath: I share my abundance with all.

(You are not an impersonal receptacle for the inflowing forces of Light and Life. They awaken your awareness of your higher nature; what you have received is now *your* abundance. You share it with all; thus you are ready to receive again and to continue the endless circulation within the Whole.)

Or, again —
On an in-breath: Joyous inspiration.
On an out-breath: Joyous participation.
(The experience of life in its purity, when nothing hinders or modifies it, is *joy.* The affirmation of joy in these mantrams thus declares the high spiritual source of our *inspiration* — of which our physical inbreathing is a symbol — and of our consequent spiritual sending-forth.)

A self-explanatory pair of mantrams:
On an in-breath: Love inflowing.
On an out-breath: Love returned.

And a single-word example:
On an in-breath: Energy.
On an out-breath: Ecstasy!
(To draw in cosmic energy for our activities is a very real and valuable way to avoid overtaxing our own resources. If, however, after taking in energy we gave back only energy, our function in

the universe would be merely mechanical. It is our business not simply to replicate but to transmute: by our own inner transmutation to "set up a ferment" in our whole sphere of influence. Hence "Energy — Ecstasy!")

You'll find, besides the deep insights you gain directly from your meditations, your outlook on life as a whole will become more confident. You'll find you are less at the mercy of your own moods and of other people's. Too, your mental and psychic powers will become enhanced; they will be more effective, and will develop more rapidly than before.

An optimum time to spend in this meditation on any one occasion is around twenty minutes, although this can be extended at individual choice. When the meditation is carried out proficiently, the usual allocation of time is to spend two or three minutes in establishing Stage One, then to proceed to Stage Two and to give that two or three minutes also, before devoting the remainder of the meditation period to Stage Three.

While you are learning the formulation, however, the proportion of time given to the successive stages will necessarily vary as you give your attention to mastering one or another aspect of the meditation.

Be patient: lay the foundations well! "Simple Breathing" is perhaps a misleading title for Stage One, for the breathing itself is the least of the lesson; it is the practice of mental and bodily control which accompanies the breathing which gives this section its great value for the beginner, and to achieve this practice thoroughly is never to be completely a beginner again. It must be borne in mind, in considering this, that the procedures of this meditation are cumulative: to be sure, only two or three minutes need be given to Stage One *by itself,* but Stage One is basic to the whole formulation and its disciplines continue throughout Stages Two and Three.

In Stage Two, you should practice entering with increasing readiness into "Awareness of the Light," and holding both the breathing and the Light in consciousness throughout the rest of the meditation time. In Stage Three, the mantrams are added in (the normal procedure is to choose one's mantrams beforehand). The desirable thing is to be able to let one's mind dwell on their significance, now in one aspect, now in another, without either the breathing or the Light being lost from consciousness meanwhile.

Every individual is free to organize the personal meditation period according to his or her own needs during the learning process; but it can be considered a sign of proficiency when the stages flow smoothly one from another, and when the time-scale works out approximately as given above.

With regard to *physical exercise,* everyone who is able should have some kind of daily program, and there is plenty of advice to be had on this subject. You can choose whatever is best suited to your bodily needs; but, for the greatest benefit possible in connection with your psychic development program, you should favor some form of *aerobic* exercise.

Just now so many exercises are being given this name, you may not always be able to see what's essential to them. *Aerobic exercise is any exercise done so as to step up the supply of air — and, most especially, of oxygen — to the skin and muscles, thereby increasing the availability of energy throughout the body.*

Oxygen reaches the muscles not only by being carried by the blood from the lungs, but also it enters through the pores in the skin. If the skin is given no opportunity to breathe freely, both it and the whole body lose tone, suffer a depletion of energy and of elasticity. The brain and the nervous systems also suffer and their work is impeded by lack of oxygen.

This means you should choose whatever exercises you need for your individual requirements, *but do some part strenuously, raising the heartbeat to about 140 per minute for several minutes: if you are fit, five minutes or more.* Do this at a place and time which will give your lungs and skin the best breathing conditions. Slimming or muscle-building exercises, posture-aiding or just plain keep-fit exercises: all can be "aerobic" if performed vigorously with free access to good air.

So a spell of jogging-on-the-spot, for instance, lightly clad and by an open window overlooking grass, trees, a garden, is better than jogging beside the road in a sweatsuit. Also, emphatically, if you choose to jog, you should never do it alongside that road when it's busy, when you would be absorbing a lot of gasoline and diesel fumes — they're lethal!

If you must do all your exercises inside a room, okay, just do them as lightly clad as possible. Wear nothing at all, if you can. A "gymnasium" is, literally, a place for nudity. And, remember, pot-plants in a house keep the air healthy for you. (But cut flowers *don't*.) Have as many plants indoors as you can look after: they give you much more benefit than you need to give them.

Now we come to a few things you'll want for testing and for developing your psychic faculties. You can probably buy some of them if you wish to, at some bookstores which specialize in psychism or in various related subjects, but it costs less and is much more fun to make your own. Besides, they'll then be really your own, and you can take a pride in them (as you should with equipment of this kind) in a way which nothing you buy ever quite equals.

You'll need a PENDULUM. This can be made from wood or metal. Metal is popular, mainly with people who want to specialize in finding metals, but wood is to be preferred for general purposes.

PENDULUMS

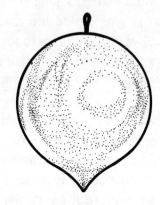

Turned wooden pendulum

Whittled wooden pendulum

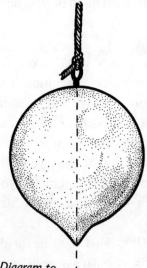

Diagram to show true balance

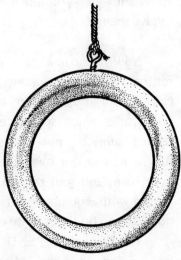

Ring-shaped pendulum

Your pendulum should be large enough to be fairly weighty, say a couple of inches in height, and may be any one of several shapes. It can be *cylindrical* or *spherical,* but in either of these forms it will be made easier to use if you give it a small basal point, so your pendulum will be about the size and shape of a small turnip, or of a large, long radish. You can turn it on a lathe, or you can whittle it from a piece of soft, even-grained wood. (Fruit-tree wood is best.) Or you can make your pendulum disc-shaped like a small clock-pendulum; or it can be ring-shaped. Although not so frequently seen at present, the ring shape, whether in wood or in metal, can give excellent results. Women through the centuries have used their wedding ring, suspended by one of their own hairs, for their personal divination. A large wooden curtain-ring is also very good, especially if you remove any paint or enamel with which it may be furnished. Such a ring sometimes has a small screw-eye already set in it at one point, and this can be used for suspending the pendulum.

If you are making your own pendulum of spherical or cylindrical shape, you'll do well to add the small screw-eye for suspension *before finishing the shaping.* That way, you can hang up the pendulum to check for any errors in balance while you can still correct them. For true balance, you should be able to look at your pendulum from any side and imagine a straight vertical line running down through cord and pendulum to the tip as the instrument hangs motionless.

The suspension is quite as important as the pendulum itself. The vital thing is not to use a twisted cord or thread, as this would influence the movement. People in past times have used one of their own hairs, as has been noted, or a long horse-hair; you can very well use a non-twisted nylon thread. Attach it to the suspension ring with a secure, simple knot, then hang up your pendulum to test it. When hanging from a peg free from vibration, it should hang straight and still.

When the pendulum is true and completed, best leave well alone. A thin film of shellac can be added if you wish, but the plain wood is most satisfactory.

Another thing you'll need is a set of E.S.P. CARDS. Customarily these cards are twenty-five in number, each one showing a shape boldly drawn in black upon white; the pack includes five shapes, each being used five times. Generally, the shapes employed are star, circle, square, cross, and wavy lines. You may want to change some of them, either for the sake of experiment or as a result of your own experience. For instance, if you and your friends often confuse star and cross, or square and circle, you might want to substitute, say, a triangle

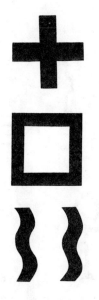

or a crescent or a diagonal bar for one or another of the standard shapes. Or you might want to have a different set of shapes altogether. One could for instance make an excellent set comprising Scarab, Djed-column, Ankh, Crook and Flail, and Eye. Whatever set of five shapes you choose, each shape should be readily distinguishable from its fellows. You can have more than one set if you like; it's your game!

Make all the cards in a set of one size, from white board or stiff plastic with the symbols painted, or cut out in black paper and glued on. For convenient handling, the cards are frequently made about the size of playing cards; for group use, especially for beginners, a larger set is better. You might make them square, five or six inches along each side, with the symbols large in proportion.

What you should NOT change is *the total number of cards in the set, and having five cards with each symbol.* The reason for this is that you may want at some time to compare your group's results with results from another group, or with data in a book. A differently constituted set of cards can defy comparison.

Later in this book we shall come to various ways these cards can be used to show different psychic powers; but when tests are made, the accepted "norm" is that a person gets five cards out of the twenty-five right. To achieve a higher score, particularly as an average figure scored over a number of tests, is taken as indicating a true psychic ability; its exact meaning of course depends on the conditions of the tests. For a person to score often *lower than* the norm is also interesting; for this too suggests there is a factor at work other than chance.

To practice *scrying*, you will need a VISION MIRROR. Scrying can be done with an ordinary mirror or with a crystal sphere; but an excellent and traditional instrument for the purpose is not in any ordinary sense a "mirror" at all, being designed to absorb, not to reflect, light which falls upon it.

This instrument is a concave disc, about eight inches across and of any depth up to hemispherical. You can make the basic structure in any way which will give a rigid, paintable object capable of being set up in an almost vertical position. Anyone with the necessary equipment can easily turn the hollow in a block of wood which has been shaped to stand in that way, or the "mirror" can be made from metal, from plastic or from papier-mache. Papier-mache has a venerable tradition in the making of occult and religious equipment, and was made and painted with great skill in ancient Egypt. The standard modern technique for making it, as usually taught in schools, will be found very suitable in constructing your Vision Mirror.

However made, the whole of the instrument except for the concave "mirror" surface is usually painted in some neutral shade such as grey. The "mirror" surface (the "inside" of the bowl) is to be finished in black gloss. Best results are obtained if the complete procedure using primer, undercoat and enamel is followed, making sure the undercoat is completely dry and smooth before finishing. The final surface is to be free from any irregularities so as to present a perfectly featureless black "hole" when in use.

(It is customary to ornament the rim of a Vision Mirror with the Signs of the Zodiac in a circle all around it. If you like this tradition, by all means follow it: if you feel it might be a distraction or would be out of place, you are free to omit it.)

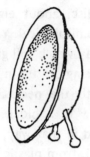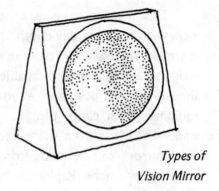

Types of
Vision Mirror

If you are starting out alone, you can see there's plenty for you to get involved in at once! People who have developed their psychic faculties without support and encouragement from others often go a long way, through their own determination and the fascination of the subject; but bringing your friends into your projects, if you can, will make everyone's progress easier, more interesting and altogether more rewarding.

People DO help each other psychically, not only by giving friendly encouragement, but also simply by being present and involved. *We are all much less isolated from one another than we feel,* and in psychic matters this truth becomes very evident. You and your friends will probably each, individually, have a different "best" psychic faculty; when you pool your interests and activities, each of you will naturally step up the others' ability to some extent in his or her own particular psychic talent.

There are some things in the world — knowledge is one of them and this is another — *in which you can share what you have with others, and still have just as much yourself.*

Get your friends who are interested also to make their own pendulum, ESP cards, and Vision Mirror; not all at once, but quite early in the program. You might all make your pendulums, for instance, at the same time so you can compare notes about progress. Then everyone will have good things for private practice as well as for group fun. People are generally keen to make good use of something they've created themselves, and this brings even more pleasure and enthusiasm into the program.

You'll also need to keep a log-book, a record of all the meetings of your group; if several members like to keep their own notes too, so much the better! More about records later.

Checkpoint

1

- Bend down and touch your toes, as described in the text —
  (a) Really meaning it and expecting success.
  (b) As if you don't expect success.

  You can tell how different these two performances feel, and how different the results are. Reflect upon the great influence of your psyche, even in a simple bodily exercise.

- Get your friends to join you in the development of psychic powers. But don't be too serious — these powers are best developed in PLAY.

- Do everything towards your psychic development program with *imaginative enthusiasm*. Make this a habit, now and for the future!

- Make your body as fit and healthy as you can.

- Plan yourself a sound healthy diet, including plenty of raw foods such as salads and granola.

- Whenever you are not actively using your body, rest and relax it. Learn to relax mentally too.

- Become proficient in the Tabor Formulation, and employ it every day. Remember, psychic development sessions should always be preceded by this meditation.

- Exercise your body; aerobic exercise is best, but do it in conditions where good oxygenization can result.

- Have green plants growing in the house; they help give you good air.

- Acquire these, preferably making them yourself:
    A pendulum
    At least 1 set of ESP cards
    A Vision Mirror.

- Keep a log-book; use it to record all activities which you and your friends organize to develop your psychic powers.

Study Points
2

1. Psychic Powers are a natural part of you, and while they are not a sign of "high sanctity," their development is a reflection of your attitude towards life in general. Cultivating an "openness" toward all life is an important part of your program.

2. All Psychic Powers are manifestations of Life—
   as movement,
   as forms of energy,
   as a reaching out towards other manifestations of life or of energy.
   a. Reaching out to the Natural World.
      People who are in intimate contact with Nature often become highly psychic. Ways in which Nature Contacts are cultivated are part of many systems of magical and religious training.

b. Reaching out to the Human World.

Genuine interest in the people you know, and even in those you see around you, fosters understanding and psychic relatedness.

c. Reaching Within.

Inner Peace is the basis of a most important factor in psychic practice—the "letting-go principle" — which is also part of the "relaxed attentiveness" that works to free psychic channels from the stress that can inhibit psychic abilities. *All your psychic practice should be done without a feeling of "pressure for result."*

3. The Unconscious levels of your psyche have access to untold resources of knowledge, to which your conscious mind alone has no key. Methods to set the unconscious self to gain knowledge and comprehension are important parts of your psychic development program.

a. A feeling of focus for the "physical attention" with the 'psychic attention" kept *free and poised* should be cultivated.

b. Systems of divination—such as the use of the pendulum described in this chapter—will help build a "code" that the Unconscious can accept for communicating with your conscious mind.

4. Time is a condition of the Material Universe: the world of the psyche is not bound by the time limita-

tions of the material world. Testing — as with the ESP cards as described in this chapter — can reveal "time-slip" as when a person perceives past or future events.

5. Testing is an important part of your program for developing your psychic powers. But, over-testing should be avoided, for it can lead to boredom, and *boredom is death to psychism!*
   a. Psychism flourishes best in an atmosphere of adventure, discovery and delight.
      Group testing can build an overall atmosphere helpful to all the participants.
      Solitary testing should be undertaken in a spirit of enthusiasm, patience, and endless curiosity.
   b. This chapter starts a program of both group and solitary testing that will both reveal "native" psychic abilities and encourage their development.

6. In your psychic practice, do not be discouraged by the "anti-psychic" attitudes of others. The truly scientific attitude means that you should follow wherever the evidence leads — without prejudice that limits your perception of, or acceptance of, the results of experiment or observation.

2
Exploring Your Potential

Your psychic faculties are a natural part of you, and to use them in play is the surest method to develop them. So anyone who follows out the suggestions in this book is going to have good results, especially when directing their diet, rest and exercise along the lines we've suggested, CREATIVELY. But for *best and most lasting results* there's something further you should consider, not just while you are a beginner but for always. It's really a common-sense part of a psychic development program.

Your attitude to life in general.

This is so important that we have to say something about it. Your attitude and way of life may already be excellent, yet you may not have realized how important it is to your psychic development program.

Certainly, research indicates the best possible attitude of mind for psychic development is one of serious attentiveness combined with relaxation, an inner feeling of happiness and interest *and a frequent renewal of attention*. Boredom, stress and prolonged concentration are alike to be avoided. Certainly too, this view is supported by the "casuality lists" of professional ESP testing over the years: the innumerable outstandingly psychic people tested to a standstill, sometimes for life, at universities and research centers. Which is why we say,

DON'T OVER-TEST – HAVE FUN!

Your psychic abilities are all manifestations of LIFE, manifestations which exist as movement, as forms of energy, as a reaching out towards other manifestations of life or of energy.

So, now and always, encourage the development of those faculties by doing some deliberate reaching out.

(a) Reaching out to the natural world

People who live continually in contact with the natural world often become highly psychic. To sleep under the stars, if only for seven or even three nights, will for many people act as a "crash course" to step up their general psychic perceptions; and in various religious systems — African and Native American religions providing well-known examples — people at some spiritual crisis undergo a stay in the wilderness, where a personal vision or revelation is to come to them.

Young people about to cross the bridge into adult life are frequently given an experience of this kind; men and women entering into a state of priesthood in those religions have, traditionally, more severe trials during their separation from the community. Always, this experience which deepens the life of the individual is intended to transcend the material world and to confer a permanent link with the world of spirit.

If you can reach out into the natural world in the context of your own religious faith, you should do so; most religions indicate that we should find the signature of the Eternal in the works of nature, and this should be a particularly joyful aspect of faith. If, however, you do not have a religious motivation but seek psychic renewal and growth simply as part of your human heritage, you need another line of approach, to prevent your either falling victim to tedium or seeking too anxiously for your psychic prize.

IT'S NO USE SITTING ON A HILL WONDERING MO-MENT BY MOMENT IF YOU ARE ABOUT TO DEVELOP POWERS OF PROPHECY OR SPOON-BENDING.

Far better go backpacking with your friends who are pursuing the psychic faculties along with you; if you can't make more than one night of it, have that, and choose a beautiful and secluded spot for camping. Eat sparingly if at all before sleeping, but have an early and hearty open-air breakfast.

For a long-term link with the natural world, you should take up a definite hobby which will give you something to do in the outdoor world. Astronomy or fossil-hunting, bird-watching or gardening, there are a great range of possibilities among which you can find something fascinating which is within your personal possibilities. Whatever time you spend outdoors in this way, the greater part of it should be devoted to your hobby; only stop now and then, appreciating it all from the sky above to the ground underfoot, or dwelling on some particular aspect of wonder or of beauty which strikes you. In this way, without stress or strain, you will steadily fulfill your underlying purpose.

Besides establishing your spiritual contact with and through the natural world, you should also reinforce your bonds with the human world. Much of your psychic practice is likely to be with other people; and to strengthen the general foundation of unity will, clearly, facilitate the use of your psychic powers.

(b) Reaching out to the human world

BE INTERESTED in people! This does need saying. Those of us who have an innate pull towards developing our psychic powers are as varied as any other collection of humans, and while some spontaneously have an intense interest and curiosity about every man, woman and child they meet, others only want the power to "get away from it all" so they can explore distant regions of the universe.

Exploring other planets, for example, is a real, valid and fascinating use of psychic powers, and some people's psychic findings have been considerably verified by science.* But *the higher a tree grows, the greater roots it needs;* your earthly and human basis is essential to you whatever you want to do.

So strengthen your human contacts *now.* Never mind about the number of your acquaintances, what matters is your genuine interest in the people you know.

It may be you have no problems here, or maybe you get on well with people but at a superficial level. Genuine interest may start a real friendship; always it fosters understanding and a psychic relatedness.

Consciously or not, people often give opportunities for real interest. When they show you pictures taken on their family vacation, for instance, or at their sister's wedding, it usually isn't only so you can say "What fine children," or "What a lovely dress." It's also done so as to let you into part of their lives, so you can see them not just sitting at a desk or driving a truck, but as 3-D persons with *these* relatives, *this* home, enjoying *that* relaxation. You not only see what Joe or Judy's kids look like; you can know, and understand, that much more of the real Joe or Judy.

---

*A highly interesting report of this kind, verified by Mariner 10's data on Mercury, is given in *Psychic Experiences: E.S.P. investigated* by Ostrander & Schroeder (Stirling, N.Y. 1977). Osborne Phillips, using a Qabalistic technique, had a series of similarly vivid experiences of the planet Mars, which were verified subsequently by data from the Viking spacecraft.

So reach out, in your turn, to take the offered relatedness a stage further. If Judy's sister got married, for instance, don't just say "What a lovely dress!" Add something like, "Is she going to live near you?" — something which will open a way for further communications.

(There are people, of course, that you have to be wary of. If a person asks your advice, and you give it, but then you find the same conversation is taking place over and over without really any change in the situation — that's a danger sign! The door isn't really open and you will do neither that person nor yourself any good by spending time that way. You should make a clean getaway and find other people to talk to.)

"Being a good listener" brings many rewards, and one of the greatest is the way even total strangers will feel a glow of human warmth in your company. *That glow is a real psychic rapport!* But few people realize how much the development of a good listener depends on the art of cueing others in, ensuring they'll give you something *to listen to*.

There are more ways, too, you can extend your psychic links with others. You'll notice people in a store maybe, or anywhere you happen to be. Do you wonder about them, about their lives, or make up a story, or at least a brief explanation, for the way they look or for something they chance to be carrying? If you do, you'll probably never know whether your story was right or wrong, but it's very effective practice.

While on the subject of establishing a psychic rapport with others, remember your nearest and dearest! Turn your mind sometimes to what they may be thinking, feeling, doing at the moment. In this case, you may sometimes be able to find out afterwards what they were really occupied with at that time. But don't be too serious, or make them feel uncomfortable about it, *for your own sake as well as for theirs.* It's only fun, and no harm done if you guessed wrong. And if you guessed right, that's just good fun too, and should make for a good feeling of understanding.

Don't forget here, the saints and mystics with the greatest psychic powers have always been the ones to say these powers were of "no importance." (Of course we read also of their making very good use of their abilities, to save the life of someone falling off a tower for instance, or to provide food for starving friends, or to know important news before it arrived!) But one thing they meant was that a craving for psychic powers ought not to disturb your peace of mind, or make you unhappy or solemn. And certainly it shouldn't, for any inward conflict is the surest way to be put off the track of psychic achievement.

Another thing they wanted to say was, these powers are no sign of "high sanctity" or even of having lived a life of painful austerity. We can endorse that too: psychic powers are *everyone's* natural heritage, and the only reason we have to make an effort for them is that we've regrettably grown so far away from them!

(c) Peace within ourselves

None of the other aids to psychic attainment, how-ever important, can be a substitute for this one. What it is we need to give us that inner state of serenity will differ from person to person; the gambler and the saint are unlike in character and in objective, though there may well be something of the mystic about them both. Each, too, must have a personal technique of freedom from anxiety. In between those two diverse types of psychic achiever there are people in all walks of life who, by religion or philosophy or occult understanding, or from an inborn sense of rightness and balance, possess also the secret of heart-peace.

Perhaps the best way to grasp it is TO KNOW IT IS THERE ALREADY, ALL THE TIME. Perseverance in the Tabor meditation can help you realize this.

This inner peace is the basis of a most important factor in psychic practice, which varies in its mode of application but which can, generally, be called the "letting-go principle." On embarking on any psychic practice, you need, certainly, a clear idea of what you mean to achieve; *but once you set about the proce-dure, your attitude should be a relaxed attentiveness to the procedure for its own sake, with no anxious looking for the outcome.* References to this attitude will occur here and there in this book, but you should cultivate it generally in relation to the whole of your psychic devel-opment program.

Group Tests with ESP Cards

The first thing you and your friends will want to do, when you have your material aids (or some of them) is to make a few tests to see what abilities you start out with. The record sheet for ESP card tests is to be found in Appendix A. Each person can be given six runs-through of the ESP cards: three in which the operator, the person giving the test, sees the face of the card before the call is made, and three *without the operator seeing it before all the cards have been called (pure ESP):* the principles are given in Appendix A.

If you have enough people in your group, try to arrange so each person receives the tests (especially the "seen card" tests) from assorted "operators." You may find some people get a notably higher score when calling the cards seen by one operator, than for another operator. If several people's scores favor one and the same operator, he or she may be a gifted "telepathic sender;" if there is not this agreement, but certain people score noticeably higher together than with other partners, here you may have what are called "psychic twins," even if they've never seen each other before. (Psychic twins, like natural twins, can be both of one sex or one of each). Of course these abilities and affinities need further testing and, more important, developing; but where they are found they help give interest and identity to your group, and they smooth out some statistical problems you might have later if you hadn't noticed the pattern.

Individual Tests with ESP Cards

If you are starting out alone or if you want to test your ESP in private before seeing how you compare with your friends, there are a few ways you can set yourself some "pure ESP" tests. (Solitaire telepathy with ESP cards is advanced transdimensional stuff!)

You can make yourself a card-holder and use it, as directed in Appendix A for "cards unseen" testing. Or shuffle your deck of ESP cards and, holding them face downwards, scatter them over a table; then take any card at random, guess what it is, and write down your guess before looking. Whichever way you do it, it's for several reasons best to make guesses for a number of cards before looking; put carefully in order the cards you've used, and list your guesses similarly.

Set out your results properly on ESP test sheets, again as in Appendix A. Further on in this chapter it's shown how prediction effects can appear in ESP card tests when they are set out in this way. This is quite as applicable to individual self-testing as to group activities, and when from time to time you look back over your results you should be able to discover some interesting facts about your powers and progress.

But don't be continually filling out test sheets! Over-testing threatens solitary learners more than groups. Make a point of guessing other things besides ESP cards: ball-game scores, how many phone calls you'll receive today, anything which interests you. That's a good way to build up your abilities.

Tests with the Pendulum
A — Telekinesis Testing
(Suitable for group and individual use)

You should devise a rigid arm, frame or arch, which can stand on the table so that the pendulum can hang upon twelve to eighteen inches of its cord, with nothing to prevent its moving freely and in full visibility to about sixty degrees out of vertical in any direction.

For normal use the pendulum is suspended from a person's fingers, but there are instances — as in the present test — when any reasonable possibility of movement being transmitted to the pendulum through the cord is to be prevented. The test person, seated in front of the pendulum and about three feet from it, is by psychic means to make it move in a given direction, say swinging from side to side.

Telekinesis can be used in many ways. In Chapter 3 a game will be given which is, as one of its psychic aspects, concerned with the power to influence the fall of dice; likewise, by contrast, the description is quoted of a psychic moving a handkerchief from a table under strict test conditions. For this test, however, we have chosen the pendulum because it can be seen during the action, and also because the virtual absence of friction lets it be easily moved.

Seated before the pendulum, you look at it and know you are there to move it *and you will move it* in a specific direction. When you have thought this,

you should relax in mind and body — remember the
letting-go principle — and attend to *the procedure for its
own sake, with no anxious looking for the outcome.*

Now, calmly and in joyful confidence, rest your
attention upon the pendulum: not on its surface only,
but absorbing and being absorbed by its 3-D reality as
if you loved it.

Next comes a sequence of action which must be
kept in harmony with what has gone before. *Still maintaining your relaxation, therefore,* begin a process of visualization, "seeing" the pendulum as moving though it
is still stationary. Imagine the movement without anxiety,
without trying to "pressurize" the pendulum itself. Be
patient! — build it up for some time.

Now begin to "feel" the movement (in your solar
plexus or at the back of your neck) rhythmically and
evenly while you continue to visualize it also. Let this
imagined swinging proceed, its momentum building up
in yourself, until the pendulum at which you are gazing
quivers and begins to move . . .

When good results are obtained with this test, it
can become a game. You can set the pendulum moving,
then try your power to *stop* it; next, to *change its direction.* A group can have fun, two people or teams trying
to send the pendulum opposite ways.*

---

*An account is given in Chapter 3 of the inner "mechanism" of telekinesis,
and of the area of psychic development to which it belongs. That would be
out of place with these preliminary tests, in which people are simply trying
their initial powers in some of the things there are to do, and finding the
enjoyment of doing them.

B — Pendulum Divination Tests

The next tests relate to answering questions by the use of the pendulum. Here the pendulum will be suspended, not from a frame but from the fingers, *and now it must not be prompted to move by visualization or any other means at our disposal!*

THIS IS WHERE YOU BEGIN TO ESTABLISH A NEW AND SUPREMELY IMPORTANT RELATIONSHIP WITH THE UNCONSCIOUS LEVELS OF YOUR PSYCHE.

The unconscious levels of your psyche have access to untold resources of knowledge, to which your conscious mind alone has no key. By whatever method you can set your unconscious self to gain information and comprehension for you, this is a potent and entirely authentic means of enriching your mental life. Such divinatory techniques as this use of the pendulum can give you a method of establishing a "code" which, with patient use on your part, your unconscious self will accept for communicating with you.

Pendulum Divination Tests 1: Group Testing

For the preliminary tests, people should work in twos as in the ESP card tests. In this case, one asks the questions, the other holds the pendulum by its cord and waits for a definite movement to develop so as to obtain the answers. Unlike the card tests, however, this requires some time to be put in beforehand to decide on the questions.

For this first test, it will be sufficient if each person is asked twenty questions; that is, ten to which the questioner knows the answer, and ten to which nobody knows the answer and the questioner will only discover it after a reply has been given. All twenty questions prepared for each answerer should be geared for a plain yes-or-no reply.

(This means the second ten will include such questions as, "When I cut the deck of ESP cards, will the card shown be a Square?" or, "Does this book of matches contain an even number?" — *nobody having looked.*)

At the time of this first pendulum test, it's advisable to establish for the whole group, for present and future use, agreed ways for the pendulum to signal "yes" and "no." A good plan is to understand it as "yes" when the pendulum moves forward and back, "no" when it moves from side to side.

DECISIONS OF THIS SORT, ONCE MADE, SHOULD NOT BE CHANGED, AS THAT COULD RESULT IN LASTING CONFUSION.

This still allows for the pendulum to swing in either way, or to circle clockwise or counter-clockwise, as may be significant or convenient in other contexts; it is only when a yes-or-no question is asked that the fixed form of reply should always be assumed.

Test results are set out for each person in a similar way to ESP card records (see Appendix A), and need not include a list of the questions used.

A quiet, dreamy attentiveness is the ideal emotional state for obtaining valid responses from the pendulum, and the participants in a group which is occupied in this way should be able to build up an overall "atmosphere" which is helpful to all. The mind of the person who is to give answers should focus itself upon the gentle movement of his or her pendulum. Unobtrusive, soothing background music at the beginning of the session can be recommended; it would however become a distraction if continued for too long. The feeling of the person holding the pendulum should be that the physical consciousness is limited to the arc of the pendulum's swing, while the psychic attention is poised and free.

This is, or can easily pass into, a state of light trance — an excellent condition for receiving communications from the Unconscious.

Pendulum Divination Tests 2: Individual Testing

The lone pendulum operator has, in general, an advantage; the pendulum is by its nature a one-person instrument, and the "quiet, dreamy attentiveness" mentioned above as ideal for using this instrument is, *with practice,* easier to slip into in solitude. In the early stages, however, the collective "atmosphere" of the group endeavor is a decided advantage to the participants. The solitary needs great enthusiasm, patience and above all endless curiosity to build up a similar atmosphere in the place of operation.

Much of section 1 above applies to group and "loner" alike. To find test questions whose answers are unknown to anyone poses no great problem. The ESP cards can be introduced to provide some "unknowns"; there are, too, such materials as the results of coming events, and such questions as "Do the digits on my odometer add up to. . . ?" Questions with answers known to others may be harder for the solitary pendulum operator to organize; but some at least can be planned—even questions with verifiable answers!

Two skills a group can now test, with a more expansive feeling, are the abilities to create, and to perceive, psychic images:

Mind Painting
(A group testing game)

Let everyone, with pen and paper, stand in a part-circle facing a blackboard, a television screen (blank of course) or any fairly large, dark surface.

The person at one end of the line starts off by visualizing as clearly as possible a simple shape; it can be one of the ESP shapes or any other. Having stabilized it, he or she says or signals "Okay," and tries to "project" it on to the dark surface.

(This means that having begun by "seeing" the image as if it were just in front of the center of the forehead, the person mentally "throws" it so as to "see" it, instead, in white on the dark surface. *An important tip is not to let the mind wander at that point!* Don't have anything in your mind except the shape you are sending — forget anyone else is present!)

Now everyone writes down as the first item on their list, *without saying anything,* what they themselves can "see" on the board. *Ten seconds only are allowed for doing this.* (The "sender" should write it too, to record what it was.) Some people may really "see" as if with their eyes; others may get a mental realization, a belief as to what they would have "seen" if they "saw." Others may get a word, or a feeling. Whatever each one gets or seems to get *must be written down in ten seconds.* Then the next person in line visualizes an image of his or her own choice, says or signals "Okay," and "projects" the image on to the dark surface. Everyone looks, and the result is added to their list as Item 2. Now it's the third person's turn.

When everyone has had their turn, the lists should be read out. You score one point for each of your correct answers on images sent by other people. You get no point for the right answer on your own paper for the image *you* sent! — but you get a point for each other person who has it right. *So a right answer scores for the player who "sees" it correctly, and for the sender.*

Thus if there are five people playing, the highest possible score is *eight:* four points for naming all the other players' images rightly, and four more if they all named your image rightly. If there are ten people playing, the highest possible score is *eighteen.*

The ability to project an image clearly is a valuable one, and although not highly developed in many people at first, it can be highly trained with practice in exact formulation. Many people, however, seem to have without any training the ability to "see," at least in general terms, an image sent by an able sender; on occasion they may do so without realizing that what is seen *is* a projected image.

For example: three young women who often amused themselves with collective psychic games, one evening were traveling some distance on a subway train. During the early part of their journey there were many empty seats, and as a pastime they built up an imaginary fellow-passenger sitting in one of the seats opposite.

As they approached the city center, the train became more and more crowded until a lot of people were standing for lack of seats — but until the three reached their destination, *nobody made a move to sit in the seat which had the imaginary occupant!*

Look Again at Test Results!

In the next chapter we shall be considering the ways in which different psychic aptitudes can be associated with each other. But from the beginning, as you look at the test and game scores obtained by yourself and your friends, you should look not only for what the test or game is designed to show, but also for other aptitudes it suggests. (People who are good with visualized images may also be good scryers.)

One thing you ought to watch for in all test records is the psychic who gets "wrong" answers which are due to being out of step, time-wise. Time is, as we can easily understand, very much a condition of the material universe; we measure it by movements in the solar system, or by clocks or other instruments, or by our own heart-beats. We need to find out when to eat or sleep or work, when to plant crops or to go on vacation. The world of the psyche is bound by no such measurements, and no such needs.

Notably with the ESP cards, but also with pendulum and "vision" tests, it can occur that a person is one or even two steps behind, or before, the question. That's why it is best, whenever possible, for answers only to be disclosed to the person being tested *after the whole test is over*. It's also the reason why, when the cards are being called *unseen by the operator*, they should be stacked carefully in order, still face downwards, and not be seen BY ANYONE until the test is ended. Say for instance we have this result:

	Card	Call
1	Square	W.Lines
2	Circle	Square
3	Star	Circle
4	Circle	Star
5	W.Lines	Star
6	Cross	W.Lines

— when the cards are being called "unseen."

If at *no* stage during the test the operator had seen these cards, the result would represent a noteworthy example of TIME-SLIP. If however, *as soon as the subject had made each call,* the operator looked at the card, the result we have would probably be due to telepathy, the subject frequently calling the symbol at which the operator had just been looking. The break in the pattern at the fifth call might then be due to the operator having glanced at the second Circle in the series, thinking "We just had one of those"; the subject, picking up the thought, will have reacted by repeating the Star. The importance should be obvious, of examining both test conditions and results so as to see what psychic qualities are truly being revealed.

Foreknowledge is Demonstrated

A different kind of problem sometimes besets people when time-slip goes the other way, so that the test results demonstrate *prescience* (foreknowledge).

Prescience is simply a fact which, in the annals of ESP, has been established again and again. Yet some people — who pride themselves on their "scientific" approach — still make problems about accepting its reality, *and for a totally unscientific reason.* They want facts cut down to size, to save their theories.

If you want to be really scientifically minded in whatever may be your line, whether it's archeology, agriculture or psychism, you must be ready to follow wherever the evidence may lead.

The "anti-prescience" attitude is basically this:

Prescience implies that the future exists now.
This implication is objectionable.
Therefore, prescience does not occur.

That line of "reasoning" is open to question from beginning to end!

What kind of "existing now" of the future is necessary to prescience?

To whom is it objectionable or inconceivable?

And finally, may we say something is true *only if we fully understand it? (Or approve it?)*

Usually in the history of mankind, discovery of what exists has come first. Explanations come much, much later, if at all.

We still can't totally explain electricity. We are still researching the origins of Native American peoples and cultures. Even the full story of why we go to sleep is uncertain, but we go on doing it.

So now and then people catch glimpses of the future, whether of an international crisis or of the next ESP card to be turned up. People sometimes have prophetic dreams. People sometimes utter a prophetic speech, without any idea why they say it, without even believing it. *This points to the action of unconscious levels of the psyche. Isn't that the more reason why we should open communication with those levels?*

You have a whole new world to discover and to explore—the wonderful and immense world of
YOUR POTENTIAL
And besides, the experience and understanding which your psychic development activities are going to bring you will fundamentally enhance the quality of
YOUR LIFE IN THIS WORLD

Checkpoint

2

- The best attitude of mind for psychic development combines serious attentiveness with relaxation. *To be avoided* are boredom, stress and intense concentration alike!

- Your contacts at all levels are vital.
    Establish and keep your contacts with the world of nature.
    Establish and keep your contacts with the world of people.
    Establish and keep peace in your own heart.

- Make the "letting-go" principle your own: decide your objective clearly, then keep a relaxed attentiveness to the procedure for its own sake, with no anxious looking for the outcome!

- Have your friends join in tests with ESP cards, for telepathy and for "pure ESP."

- Your pendulum is great —
    Suspended from a frame, for telekinesis.
    Hand-held, for answering questions.

- Establish a new relationship: learn wonderful things from your psyche's unconscious levels!

- "Mind painting" — enjoy it as a test or as a game. You score points for success, both in sending visualized images and in receiving them.

- Don't over-test — but DO return to testing techniques as valid development material in their own right. *It's the spirit that counts!*

- Two maxims from this chapter:
    DON'T OVER-TEST: HAVE FUN!
    As a researcher —
    FOLLOW THE EVIDENCE
    WHEREVER IT LEADS!

- Keep up the Tabor Formulation at least once a day.

Study Points
3

1. The Psyche is your non-material self . . . . but it is also a far vaster reality than the "I" consciousness with which we explore it. In addition, the Psyche has entry into the Collective Unconscious of the human race, and, further, into that of all Life.

2. The Psyche can interact with matter and with other psyches, and these two capabilities — along with the various "internal powers of the psyche" — are the basis of most psychic abilities.

3. The human psyche has four main levels of function:
   a. The Spirit—
      which is your Higher Self, a part of the world of the Divine, and the ultimate source of your true inspiration and guidance.

   b. Mental Level—
   including the conscious rational mind. It receives
   information from the emotional & instinctual level
   and directives from the Spiritual level.
   c. Astral Being—
   including the emotional and instinctual level. At
   its higher level it is conscious and engages with
   the mind, and at its lower level is unconscious
   and engages with the life functions of the physical
   body. It also has access to the content of the
   Collective Unconscious.
   d. The Physical Body —
   including the cerebro-spinal and autonomic
   nervous systems, and the digestive and glandular
   organs, all of which interact with the emotional &
   instinctual level. It is the physical body which is
   the "instrument" of your action in the physical
   world.

4. Every Psychic Power originates in the Astral level
   of the psyche. It is the plan of this book to develop
   these powers, to bring them into consciousness,
   and to place them under control of the rational mind.

5. The increasing activities of the Astral that will occur
   in psychic development make it important that the
   natural interaction of all the levels be strengthened
   from time to time, making us more receptive to
   the inspiration and guidance of the Higher Self.

This strengthening it achieved by meditation called:
"Reflection on the Psycho-spiritual unity."
In using this procedure, regard "yourself" as identified with your conscious rational mind — which you
know to be responsible *to* your Higher Self "above"
and responsible *for* your physical body and the
emotional and instinctual level "below." The rational
mind should link the lower faculties, through itself,
to the Higher Self, thus making the Whole Person —
Body and Soul — the instrument of the Higher Self.

6. "Like acts upon like."
Although all psychic powers have their source in
the Astral level, those that interact with other
minds at a fairly high level — as in true telepathy —
operate at a higher astral level; those that interact
with ordinary emotions or the imagination, are
sent from a middle astral level; and those that act
upon the material plane are sent from a dense lower
astral level.
a. Some psychic powers involve the energy of the
Aura — which emanates continually from the astral
body. This is the basic instrument of telepathy —
for both transmitting and receiving.
b. In some cases, communication may be through the
Collective Unconscious, with its emphasis on
symbols and images.
c. In other cases psychic powers involve the projection of astral "substance." Many cases of

"spirit rappings" or spontaneous telekinesis involve an accidental ejection of astral substance.

d. In yet other cases, as in some procedures involved
in healing, both astral substance and auric energy
are used.

3

Psychic Abilities
and Mechanisms

The human psyche is defined as the non-material part of the human individual. The idea, "You have one psyche, I have another" is a true reflection of a reality: one person's psyche differs from another in emotions, inclinations, abilities, aspirations. Thus far we can think of our psyche, if we choose, as a non-material "self" formed rather like a phantom replica body.

Nevertheless, much of the psyche's experience is not "self" at all, in our usual application of that word. It is also questionable how far we "have" or "possess" the psyche; at all levels, both higher and lower, it is a vaster reality than the consciousness with which we explore it. Besides, the psyche has its mysterious doorway, hidden but never closed, into the Collective Unconscious; first, into that of the human race, and, beyond, into that of all life forces.

The psyche, by its nature, is capable of various interactions with matter as well as with non-material realities, and these two capabilities form the main heads of our inquiry. The action of the psyche upon matter (whether the person's own body or external objects), and the action of one psyche upon another, form the bases for a number of highly interesting developments and powers. Other abilities, which we may call the internal powers of the psyche, are also very well worth developing; they are less measurable, less demonstrable, but they can be of immense value in our lives. *Such is the ability to monitor our dreams, or to achieve out-of-the-body experience.**

We shall presently be examining psychic abilities and mechanisms in more detail. First, however, we shall look at the organization of the human psyche, and then we shall consider a way by which our knowledge of its structure and nature can become a vital and meaningful force within us.

The mystical tradition of the West (which has been developed from the experience of devoted adherents in many lands and ages) has consistently found in the human person four main levels of function:

---

*It is impossible, in a book combining this scope with these dimensions, to give full directions on every psychic power. We include explicit details on developing some important and topical ones; other psychic powers already have, or are intended to receive, detailed treatment in individual Llewellyn Practical Guides.

1.   *The spirit,* which is in essence divine and which is, and remains, a part of the World of the Divine. Only those who have begun high mystical development have an awareness of the presence of the spirit; but it exists in every person as the Higher Self, that supernal flame of selfhood which is the ultimate source of individuality.

2.   *The mental level of the psyche,* which includes the conscious rational mind but is not limited to it. The mental level should be, and in its rightful development is, receptive to promptings from the Higher Self; it is also receptive to impulses and attitudes from the emotional and instinctual levels, for whose welfare (with that of the physical body) it is responsible.

3.   *The Astral Level of the Psyche.* This is the emotional and instinctual level of the psyche, which in its higher range engages with the mental level, giving incentives for intellectual effort and supplying imaginative color to spiritual enterprise. In its lower range, which is largely unconscious, it participates in the life-functions of the physical body. The unconscious area of the psyche's emotional and instinctual level also affords the most usual means of access to the content of the Collective Unconscious.

Within the astral level of the psyche we discern two major regions, *the higher and the lower astral;* these are distinct in character and function (much as, for instance, are the root and the stem of a plant) without being divided by any sharp line of demarcation.

These two regions merge into one another by impercep-
tible degrees: the dense or lower astral which is nearer
to the physical body and acts more in conjunction with
that, being the domain of the instincts and of the supportive life-processes, and the fine or higher astral which
is nearer to the rational mind and acts more in conjunction with that, being the domain of the higher emotions.

   The psychic powers have their foundation in the
astral level of the psyche. In primitive life the use of
many of these powers was probably directly connected
with the instincts (as for example the power to find
water when thirsty, or the power to communicate by
telepathy with fellow-members of a foraging party) and
would be activated without conscious volition when need
arose. For most people within our civilization nowadays
these powers have become more or less submerged
by disuse, but they are intrinsic to human nature, and
are capable of being reawakened.

4.   The physical body, including the cerebro-spinal
and autonomic nervous systems, as well as the digestive
and glandular organs, all of which interact with the
emotional and instinctual level of the psyche to an
important but variable extent.

   This, then, is the basic structure of the human
entity throughout the levels of its being. Now that
the psychic faculties are to be developed, thus
increasing astral activity in particular, the natural interaction of all the levels needs from time to time to be
strengthened, so that imbalance may be prevented and

the whole person benefit to the maximum. In regard to the Higher Self, we shall be making ourselves by this means more aware and effective recipients of its inspiring and guiding forces.

This implementation of our knowledge is achieved by a meditative process we call "Reflection on the Psycho-physical Unity."

When using this procedure, you should regard "yourself" as identified with your conscious rational mind, which is your focal point and center of responsibility; it is responsible *for* your body and the emotional and instinctual level of your psyche, which are "below" it, and responsible *to* your Higher Self which is "above."

Reflection on the Psycho-physical Unity

This procedure is not meant to be part of your daily program, and IN NO CASE should it be combined or confused with the Tabor Formulation. *Nor is it intended for group use: here you meet yourself.*

It should be done about once a week, in bed at night before you sleep. It can also be done any time you need it or would find it refreshing or inspiring, lying down or seated in any easy comfortable posture. Its performance is not a matter for acquiring exactness or discipline; if for instance you happen sometimes to fall asleep during it, there's no harm done. But it should always be regarded as a voyage of adventure and self-discovery, a true exploration of the psyche.

The meaning and direction of the text does need to be understood. For this purpose you should read it through a few times before trying it, and in the early stages of its use keep your reflections fairly simple and not too long.

The subject matter given below is divided into four categories, which you should go through in succession during your meditation. When you begin the procedure, let your mind dwell on the first category for as long as subject-matter arises to your consciousness, then go on to the second category, dwell on that in the same way, and so proceed. Don't deliberately visualize, and don't strive for intellectual lines of thought; just let your mind explore at its leisure whatever aspects it finds within, or arising from, the given areas of material.

If at any point your mind encounters any painful reflection, you should try neither to repress this nor to dwell on it needlessly. The intention should be to recognize the true facts of whatever is found painful, then to move on to other aspects of the material, so that without rejecting the painful aspect you may help yourself to see it in the wider perspective of the whole meditative process.

The sequence of subject-matter to be reviewed is as follows:

(a) Your relationship with the material world and with your body.

Reflect upon your body as the instrument of your action in the material world, and the means of your manifestation. In these two functions, the body not only merits right treatment and respect; only if given right treatment and respect is it able to serve you as it should.

Reflect upon the knowledge and the varied experience which comes to you through the five senses. Then dwell upon your relationships with the world of nature, and your responses to the magnitude and beauty of the cosmos.

(b) Your relationship with your emotional and instinctual level.

Reflect upon this, the astral level of your psyche; familiar as being the source of your emotions, cryptic and powerful as being the source of your psychic faculties.

Reflect also upon this level of your psyche as supportive to the rational mind and so to your whole being; upon the instincts as maintaining your physical life, upon such qualities as incentive, adventure, romance, which the astral nature adds to the deliberations of reason.

If we pay heed to our astral nature, it will respond. One mode of its response is through the changeful and mysterious realm of dreams.

Yet this sensitive and in some ways child-like part of ourselves requires from our rational self love and care, understanding and firm guidance. There is much matter for reflection as to

how and in what measure this responsibility is to
be fulfilled.

*(c) Your relationship with the world of the
mind.*

This includes a review of the powers of the
intellect, of the great vistas of comprehension and
of judgment to which the mental level of your
psyche is native; not only within itself, but including the immense world of thought in which
it participates. You can recognize that your brain,
nervous system, emotional nature and other circumstances place limitations which are not its
own upon your mind; the mind is, in its own
nature, essentially free and necessarily self-deter-
mining.

At the same time, your survey of it should
include a recognition that this free and, ultimately,
invincible Mind is always responsible to that
which is its origin and goal, the inmost pinnacle
of the psyche, the Higher Self or spirit.

In a certain sense, you *are* the rational mind,
and as such you are poised continually between
your Higher Self and your emotional-instinctual
nature. The way to keep this balance is to recognize
the presence of the Higher Self and to seek its
guidance. Even if to begin with you have no awareness of it, this acceptance of the right order will
lead you to develop that awareness.

(d) Your relationship with your Higher Self.

When the rational mind becomes receptive to promptings from the Higher Self, it becomes the interpreter and representative of the Higher Self to the lower faculties: that is, to the emotional and instinctual level of the psyche, and to the physical body. The responsibility of the rational mind is not simply to attach itself to the Higher Self, but to link the lower faculties, through itself, to that luminous reality which is in truth a facet of Godhead. The level of the Mind is the only level of the psyche which is capable of achieving this link, and thus aligning the whole being to the life-giving source. *The entirety of which reuniting bond, from the height to the depth, is Love.*

To return to our examination of psychic abilities. The writings of Professor Leonid L. Vasiliev, the pioneer of psychic research in Soviet Russia, are notable for their scientific precision. In an atmosphere which was at that time hostile to any evidence of the existence of mind-power, he had to take every precaution to ensure nobody could challenge his statements. In his book *Mysterious Phenomena of the Human Psyche** he relates the painstaking precautions of two French experimenters to establish the reality of the force exerted by a psychic moving an object by telekinesis.

---

*Translated by Sonia Volochova, introduction by Felix Morrow (University Books, New York 1965).

The psychic, well-known Rudi Schneider, was being tested by the director of the Paris Institute for Meta-psychology, Eugene Osty, with the help of Marcel Osty, his son. Schneider, whose hands and feet were held by the two investigators throughout the test, was seated at some distance from the table on which was the object he was to move: a handkerchief. Table and handkerchief were guarded by infra-red beams, monitored by a galvanometer; other apparatus, including a camera, was controlled by ultra-violet light.

This arrangement was made because during a previous experiment which had been geared merely to exclude trickery, the genuineness of Schneider's psychic activity had been established and the handkerchief had been moved, but there was nothing to show "how it was done." The psychic himself had stated at that time that a substance, invisible to the others but visible to himself, had been exuded from his body; he could control it, and would use it to move the handkerchief. The new experiment, with its complex equipment, was accordingly set up by the Ostys to test the objective existence of the invisible substance.

Astonishingly to the people of that time (1930-1931) the results of this test were entirely in accord with what Rudi Schneider had said. The handkerchief was moved, no visible object had approached it, *but the galvanometer recording showed that some type of palpable force had broken through the infra-red beam at the time the handkerchief was moved.*

The Ostys reported their experiments in the *Revue Metapsychique* (#6, 1931 and #1 & 2, 1932). Vasiliev expresses surprise that nobody took up the report, either to support or to challenge it, and nobody brought it to the attention of the world at large. We may think it was, perhaps, "nobody's pigeon;" the evidence of psychic power may have offended the materialists, while the evidence of the near-material nature of the force employed may have offended the upholders of psychism. At all events, this well-conducted, well-documented experiment is of very great interest to us.

Certainly the force employed by Schneider was a "psychic" force: it was not a component of his physical body. Without any reasonable doubt, it was the same as the "ectoplasm" of physical mediumship, and as the "astral substance" from which the out-of-the-body traveler creates his vehicle, or astral likeness.

This astral substance can be ejected from various regions of the body — the solar plexus and the crown of the head are frequent sites — or more rarely from all the body surface, as seems to have occurred here. It varies in density according to whether it is drawn from a higher or lower part of the astral level: for most psychic purposes the lowest levels are not employed, as so doing can cause unwelcome disturbances in the physical body. In the case under discussion, Schneider was probably employing a denser level of astral substance than was strictly needed for his purpose.

We are told his rate of breathing accelerated during these experiments to 200 — 300 per minute, *or about eighteen times the normal rate!* Other people have not found it necessary to reach such a condition before performing telekinesis or physical mediumship. There are, besides, innumerable examples of accidental ejection of astral substance to varying extents: the type of incident in which a person is scared by nocturnal "spirit rappings" which are really self-caused, or the kind of telekinesis which produces such comments as, "I only looked at that plate and it seemed to jump off the shelf!" Nevertheless, Rudi Schneider's demonstration shows us how close to the material level astral substance can be.

At the other end of the scale, we have a notable investigation, Russian this time, into the nature of *telepathy*. When Professor Vasiliev wrote the book just quoted, there was an idea that telepathy might be due to an electro-magnetic current from brain to brain.

We have to be careful here in interpreting genuine evidence. It is a fact that if electric terminals are attached to a person's head (as is often done in the professional investigation of brain activity) and a telepathic message is transmitted to that person, *some message which has real emotional significance to him or her,* the emotional reaction to that message will be recorded as an "electro-encephalogram." But it is entirely the emotion, not any supposed "telepathic current," which causes that recordable reaction.

Before proceeding, it must be recognized that for psychic fact-gathering, or for the transmission of psychic power, astral substance is not the only medium, and probably is not even the one most frequently employed. We also have the energy which composes the aura: energy which emanates continually from the astral level of the psyche, to form about the individual a dynamic force-field, an extensive psychostructure, highly sensitive to influences which impinge upon it or with which it comes into contact.

We know what wonders can be achieved in our defense by a well-fortified aura; this highly sensitive energic screen, and the forces associated with it, also form the transmitting and receiving instruments in telepathy, and the receptor for many sorts of data whose vibrations can be picked up for interpretation by the unconscious mind. Nobody knows how far it extends or can extend, but the distance is certainly great.

On looking into the specific uses of auric energy, however, from the practical viewpoint we often find both this energy *and* extruded astral substance are involved, so that it is impossible to tell which has done more to produce the results. In some cases *the effect of distance* gives us probably a workable test. In dowsing, for example, the nearer the dowser is to the object of search, the stronger the reaction, and we can thus infer that astral substance plays an important part: the same variation occurs in telekinesis, where we *know* astral substance is involved.

The different nature of telepathy was established in Russia, as we have mentioned above. The subjects were two psychics who had easily communicated with each other by telepathy in laboratory conditions. The two were sent to cities far distant from each other. Each was placed in an underground room which had been specially prepared; these rooms were totally insulated so no form of current or even such a fine material condition as radiation could pass in or out. Normal tests in telepathy between the two were performed, and their communication was shown to be undiminished and instantaneous despite both distance and insulation.

From this and other evidence, we can conclude that true telepathy is not conveyed by transfer of astral substance; it may in some instances relate to the extended aura, but is as nearly "purely mental" as a psychic function can be. (Naturally, telepathy can be aided by emotional motivation, but that is true of even the most intellectual or spiritual occupations possible to human beings.)

There is also the possibility of communication in either direction between a person and the collective unconscious. In such instances, any aspect of the collective unconscious may be involved, according to the nature of the particular case.

This phenomenon may provide an acceptable explanation when for instance there is a considerable time-lag between a message, idea or emotion being sent out by one person, and its reception in another's consciousness.

This validity explains some "ghostly" experiences, especially such as take a pivotal place in the life of the recipient; even more certainly is it the source of many powerful religious insights and experiences.

We cannot expect communication from the collective unconscious to happen lightly; it becomes probable when there is some inner need, whether consciously recognized or not. Men and women who frequently hold communication with the collective unconscious are either great seers, or, for the time being and from some especial cause, they are out of touch with humanity's more usual relationships. Such communication from or through the collective unconscious is, usually, either sought by special means, or marks some crisis, whether spontaneous or induced, in the personal life. (An example of an "induced crisis" would be the type of initiation we have mentioned, in which the candidate is deliberately separated for a period from human company. In such circumstances, communication from the collective unconscious in ancestral or even totemic form is not unlikely.)

The whole subject of the collective unconscious is fascinating, and is one which must always be borne in mind when seeking possible origins for some unexplained phenomenon. For your development program however, all you can do in regard of that great hidden reservoir of power and understanding is to keep your access to it as open as possible, through your inward and outward relationships with all life, including your own.

Going back to our consideration of other psychic means of receiving or transmitting knowledge or force, we can see that in them we have the beginnings of a framework on which we can represent our psychic faculties, grouping them to show which ones belong to the same level and therefore are likely to show most interaction.

It's a general principle that "like acts upon like." As true telepathy is sent at a high astral level, it must be received at a similar level. But if you have a twin, and you have a psychic link with that twin, then supposing you damage your foot your twin isn't likely to get an abstract telepathic thought of a damaged foot; he or she will more probably get a pain in the corresponding foot itself.

To produce effects deliberately, therefore, you must get into harmony with what you want to do.

Although all your psychic powers come from the astral region of your psyche, those which interact with other minds at a fairly high level operate from your higher astral level, those which interact with ordinary emotions or with the imagination are sent from your less elevated astral level, and those which act upon the material plane are sent from a dense astral level of your psyche. No matter how much your mental self, or even your spiritual self, is in charge of the action — as it should be — *the action itself has to take place at the appropriate level of your psyche: that is, the level which can give rise to the type of power which is to be used.*

We illustrate these relationships below by setting out some of the better known psychic powers in a table, opposite the faculties which gave rise to them. This has required some simplification; the psyche is a living, organic entity which does not function in isolated segments, so that a certain overlapping of categories is unavoidable.

Besides this, there is the imponderable factor of the *degree* to which one or another faculty is engaged in a given instance. We can say for example that some activities depend more upon auric energy, less upon astral substance; or that in one activity the astral substance employed is of a denser level than is needed in another. These are valid generalizations, although when particular cases are considered variations will be found as in any other area of nature. *We are exploring the ways in which the life-forces work, not trying to set rules and limits for them.*

Mental faculties, faculties, involving high astral level with auric perception, auric energy	Visualization, telepathy, clairvoyance, foreknowledge, scrying, psychometry
Faculties involving ejection of astral substance to some extent, and/or use of auric energy and perception	"Pure ESP," astral awareness, energy transfer, telekinesis. (*Astral Projection* is outside the series of psychic faculties described in this book.)
Receptive psychic functions involving both aura and astral body	Pendulum divination (radiesthesia), dowsing
Transensory physical or astral faculties	Eyeless sight

One interesting fact touched upon in the table is that bodily contact can in some cases yield unusual data. Some people have been able to detect whether a powder placed on the delicate skin between the fingers was sweet or salt. Vasiliev mentions a woman, and there have been many other people, able to identify colors with the finger-tips. Without actual contact, eyeless sight has on numerous occasions been performed, most usually it seems by means of the skin of the face. These things are not always "psychic" powers in the true sense of the word, but we have to take them into account as ways in which a person may obtain knowledge. In some of these instances, too, there is certainly a psychic factor involved. Well-authenticated material exists about a Brooklyn woman (Mollie Fancher) who could see from the crown of her head, and in her case we can say, from other facts about her, a use of astral substance is the surest explanation.

Another item in the table which merits special mention is the reference to "pure ESP" (psychic perception of material which has not been seen by others) being achieved *by means of some degree of ejection of astral substance* as well as by means of the aura.

In any given case, especially ones which we don't witness, we may be unable to know exactly how this feat is performed. Those who perform it may not know how they do so, for so long as we desire to achieve one of these psychic powers, and truly work for it, our unconscious mind will organize the details for us.

There are many percipients who gain a knowledge of unseen material by means only of the sensitive aura. However, supposing we know for a fact that a certain person has abilities (such as astral travel, for instance, or telekinesis) which require the projection of astral substance. In that case it would be pointless, unless we have proof, to maintain that other psychic acts performed by the same person (and perhaps on the same occasion) were done entirely *without* the aid of astral substance. The high probability is that having acquired this ability, whether consciously or not, the person employs it whenever it will be useful.

In *The Llewellyn Practical Guide to Astral Projection* you can read of a trained technique, "The Formula of the Watcher," in which, by serious intention and exact procedure, astral substance is sent forth to collect observations. In this present book, by contrast, we are primarily concerned with works which, if you do but fulfill certain conditions, your unconscious mind will carry through for you. Here we have games and a lighter atmosphere; for we are dealing with psychism, which flourishes on liberality and is often stifled by being "over-channeled." Yet here too we shall find psychic perception in association with extrusion of astral substance.

The ability to influence the fall of dice is, plainly, a form of telekinesis. And earlier in this chapter we have cited an important experiment, which relates telekinesis to extrusion of astral substance.

So now here's a game in which, experience shows, as interest mounts and energy circulates more freely, two significant things happen: the players throwing dice tend more often to make the throws they predicted, while the other players, though the dice are then unseen even by the thrower, tend to improve in ability to say if the prediction has been fulfilled.

The situation is typical for spontaneous release and return of astral substance. Pulse and breathing accelerate, temperature rises, absorption in the play-activity becomes intense. The players, who in any case will be seated fairly close together around the table, will draw involuntarily even nearer towards center, any astral substance which has been released uniting them in heightened emotional and psychic activity. This pervasive astral substance extends each person's potential for action and for perception out beyond the bounds of the physical body; but probably not beyond the limits of the game upon which each one's attention, varying only with the changes in the phases of play, remains focused.

This is an adaptation of a well-known gambling game which in its original form needs a considerable degree of skill, judgment and concentration; but none the less, even beginners often in a short time develop a real psychic flair which, in those circumstances, can make a problem! In a psychic development group, however, the simplified form given below, and its results, should be altogether congenial.

Guessing Dice

Required: Two ordinary dice, or a set of poker dice if everybody present is accustomed to them and finds them fun. A large cup for throwing. A smooth table surface. Three poker-chips (counters, toothpicks) for each player. *Players:* three or more.

We will illustrate the play first by means of the two-dice form of the game.

Say there are three players, A, B and C.

Player A begins the game by announcing what he intends to throw; for example, "Three and four."

He places the dice in the cup, shakes them, and inverts the cup over them on the table, leaving them covered.

If A is not happy about this throw, he can uncover the dice and try again; he can have up to three throws, *but whichever throw he decides is his final one must stay covered.* He then slides the cup, with the dice under it, gently to B.*

B can now reject the dice if he wishes. If he says "Challenge!" A must reveal them. If they prove to be the numbers A called, B forfeits a chip. If they do not, A forfeits. (Such chips go out of play.)

---

*When uncovering the dice (except in response to a challenge) the player should avoid letting other players see them, and should pick them up without making any comment on what he found. This will increase his psychic force, as well as keeping the others guessing as to his present abilities!

Either way, it now becomes B's turn to throw.

Or B may not wish to challenge. He may believe A made the throw he announced, or he may feel quite unsure. He decides to accept the dice.

Having accepted, B can do one of two things: (i) *Without lifting the cup*, he can slide it gently to C, saying either "Three and four," or if he feels moved to do so, some other call. Or, (ii) He can lift the cup, take up the dice, make his own call and then make a throw just as A did. B can likewise at this point make one, two or three throws (as A did), but whichever throw he decides is his final one must stay covered with the cup.

No matter what B chooses to do, when C receives the covered dice from him C can either challenge, or accept them. If C challenges and B uncovers dice which differ from the call he made, B forfeits a chip; if the dice are correct it is C who forfeits.

If C accepts, he can either pass the dice unseen to A (as next player), repeating or changing the call, or he must make his own throw or throws. The game proceeds until only one player has any chips left.

If five poker-dice are used, there are certain modifications in the game. Standard poker calls are made, 'One pair," "Two pair," etc. When second or third throws are made, one or more of the dice, *seen only by the thrower,* may be reserved under a spare cup while the thrower tries to complete the pattern of dice required by his call. But, as in the two-dice version, the throw he decides upon as the last *must remain unseen even by him*. He slides the cup or cups across to the next player, who, if making a fresh throw, will in any case employ one cup only.

In either version of the game, if at first the throwers' level of achievement is so low as to spoil the fun (if the other players can always be certain of scoring a point by challenging), a more lenient procedure may be introduced for a time: *when the dice are revealed in response to a challenge, if they represent a higher score than the one called, it is the thrower who scores, not the challenger.*

This would mean, if three and four are called while playing with two dice, then, two fours, three and five, or better, would justify the thrower; if poker dice are being used and the thrower calls a "low straight," then a "high straight" or better would count in his favor. This allowance tells us nothing about the thrower's power of telekinesis, but it helps make the game viable for beginners so they can go on playing. No matter what way this game is played, it's exciting and can do a lot for your psychic abilities!

Checkpoint
3

- "The psyche is a vaster reality than the consciousness with which we explore it."
  So explore your psyche!

- Perform the "Reflection on the Psycho-physical unity" *once a week*. Additionally to that, it should be reserved for special occasions. Make it always "a voyage of exploration and self-discovery"; its value goes beyond the context of this book, it is a friend for life.

- Check your testing arrangements for ways to add new interest. Ensure the "security arrangements" of your ESP tests.

- Some *blood-pressure monitors* have pulse readouts.

Maybe there's one around which you could use during (say) "Moving the Pendulum." Look out for any aids so you can gather more facts, enrich your records, make your sessions more fun and more really valuable. You have a *negative ionizer?* Bring it into the test room and run a "before-and-after" series of ESP tests!

• List all the questions you and your friends can think of, on how different faculties work, and plan how to get at the answers.

Study Points

4

1. Foretelling the Future — where does the information come from?

   Is it . . .

   a. Divination — communication with the Divine Mind? or. . .

   b. Seership — seeing into the Causal World where an event is formulated before it occurs in the Material World?

   The answer is that it's a little of both.

     1. An Altered State of Consciousness may bring us into contact with our own Higher Self—a part of the World of the Divine.

     2. The Astral World is causal to the Material, and levels of the psyche can contact corresponding levels of the Astral to bring through intimations of future happenings.

2. Meditation is essential to develop the ability to bring through material from the Astral.

   a. The changes in life-attitude mentioned in chapter Two — Union with the World of Nature, Union with the Human World, and Inner Peace — also help in bringing through material from the Astral.

   b. The company of others — those who have the power of prophecy — can step up your own powers.

3. Telepathy is often involved in some types of prediction:

   a. While the Unconscious Mind of the questioner often KNOWS the answer to a personal problem, it may be inhibited from transmitting its knowledge to the conscious mind because of emotional blocks. This knowledge may be picked up telepathically from the Unconscious Mind of the questioner.

   b. Sometimes it is possible to "read," through the Unconscious Mind of one person, things concerning another person with whom the first person has a psychic link.

4. Sometimes "Instinct" is the source of guidance that reflects knowledge of circumstances beyond normal means of perception — often situations of danger, or the means to satisfy hunger or thirst, etc. In some cases this may be sensitivity to "auric vibration."

5. Other material can be drawn from spiritually,

mentally or emotionally perceived implications of facts observed in the material world. Still other material may be drawn from the Collective Unconscious; this is likely to be of universal character, and to be couched in the language and symbol of folklore and religion.

6. There are many possible mechanisms at work in gaining knowledge of the future — but in cultivating your own aptitude for prophecy you can leave the "mechanics" of the process to the Unconscious Mind. However, you have to encourage the Unconscious Mind by giving it opportunities to develop its powers, as through the changes in life-style previously described, and through the fun and enjoyment of the various ESP games described in the text.

7. Scrying is one of the traditional methods by which material from the deep levels of the psyche can be made conscious.
   a. Once developed, scrying can bring answers to specific questions.
   b. In addition, delayed answers to questions asked in scrying may appear in dreams.

4

Insight &

Foreknowledge

Would you like to foretell the future?

This is generally regarded as one of the most mysterious of powers, because there has been doubt as to where foreknowledge finds that which it declares.

On this question there are two main lines of conjecture. One is that the utterer of prophecies must have direct communication with the mind of God, or of a god; hence we have such everyday words as "divination," "divining." The other view is that the soothsayer must catch glimpses of the *causal world*, where events are formulated before they occur in the material world. Thus he or she is often called a "seer," one who sees further and more significantly than many other folk; and indeed, previsions whether in sleep or in waking do often come in picture form.

The truth includes elements from both hypotheses. The astral world *is* causal to this one, although, as we know from experience, we need not and cannot regard everything which exists in the astral world as being rigidly predestined to come to pass here. And the mind with which we perceive glimpses of that world, or utter words whose meaning and motivation may be dark to us as we speak them, is certainly not our normal consciousness. When speech or sight breaks through into those other dimensions, we are to some extent "lifted out of ourselves"; this alteration may be so marked as to produce a feeling like inebriation, or it may be so slight as to pass practically without being noticed until we look back on it.

It is true to say this is the work of the unconscious mind, although the level of the unconscious mind which is involved may vary widely from seer to seer.

There are people—mystics and adepts—who can gain foreknowledge of events by catching true flashes from a facet of the Divine Mind. (Even in that case, there can still be strange confusions when human consciousness tries to reconcile the unknown with the known, the timeless with an earthly time-scale.)

Quite apart from that possibility, it is a fact that the emotional and instinctual functions of the psyche can each contact their corresponding "regions" of the astral world, and bring through some intimations of future happenings, no less than those of the past or present.

Meditation is essential to develop the power of bringing through these intimations. So are the other activities we have suggested: union with the world of nature, union with the human world, and the inner peace which is no-way diminished by your seeking for the faculties you want to develop. You should take care also to be often in the company of those who have the powers you seek; or at least, of those who likewise seek those powers. *With prophecy as with other psychic faculties, people do step up each other's powers; too, they enhance each other's willingness to speak out, which, here, is a major victory.*

The Old Testament prophets, at first glance, seem vast isolated figures, each hearkening to the divine call in his own solitude. We do not see what Isaiah the son of Amoz did before his visions came to him, nor what led up to the hand of the Lord being laid upon Ezekiel the priest among the captives in the land of the Chaldeans. We read that Jeremiah was one of a band of priests, and Daniel and his three friends had special rules of diet, but those facts might not impress us as being very significant.

It is different when we realize that in Old Testament times *prophecy was recognized as an art which could be trained. There were "schools" of prophecy.* Doubtless the students were carefully selected for aptitude. They would need, besides, years of physical and intellectual preparation for a prophet's exacting role of spiritual leadership among acute, critical people and rulers; but the psychic faculties too were developed, by methods which have been used through the ages, and everywhere, to induce ecstasy and prophetic utterance through liberation from the dominance of the intellect.

This was not every prophet's background. A noble exception was Amos the herdsman; but in his case another of our principles must be strongly emphasized, the value of a life lived in close harmony with Earth and the forces of nature.

With regard to the schools of the prophets, an instructive little picture of ancient customs, *and of their potency,* is given in the first book of Samuel.

Samuel, himself, was of a different background. In the story of his childhood we read, *the word of the Lord was precious in those days: there was no open vision.* (So, as regards Israel, we can probably date the "schools of prophets" from Samuel's lifetime, although neighboring peoples had similar traditions much earlier.) He was brought up by the priest Eli, and when he was a man *all Israel from Dan even to Beersheba knew that Samuel was established to be a prophet of the Lord.* For years, as judge, he almost ruled the nation, but when he grew old it was still as "the seer" that he was known to all. He had no objection even to being asked to divine such matters as the whereabouts of some strayed burros; and this was precisely the question Saul went to ask him, not suspecting Samuel would make him king of the land.

In Chapter 10, verses 6 and 7, Samuel is telling

Saul the happenings which are to take place during Saul's journey home:

"After that, thou shalt come to the Hill of God, where is the garrison of the Philistines: and it shall come to pass, when thou art come thither to the city, that thou shalt see a company of prophets coming down from the high place with a psaltery, and a tabret, and a pipe, and a harp before them, and they shall prophesy.

"And the Spirit of the Lord will come upon thee, and thou shalt prophesy with them, and shalt be turned into another man."

So Saul and his servant went on their way —

And when they came thither to the hill, behold, a company of prophets met him: and the Spirit of God came upon him, and he prophesied among them.

In a very real sense Saul was made for the time "another man." His everyday, reason-dominated personality was temporarily displaced while other elements surfaced, called forth in him as in the members of the company by rhythm and chant, the zither (psaltery), small drum (tabret), pipe and harp and by all the atmosphere of prophecy. These men were, undoubtedly, dancing too as they trooped down the hill, for dance in Eastern and other cultures has ever been the ecstatic companion of music and song. Dervishes, Shamans, Native Americans, Voodooists and many others throughout the world make evident the wide range of experiences which can come out of religious song and dance, from enthusiastic devotion to full trance and possession.

We are not told whether any of the prophecies made by Saul on that day were fulfilled; *they may well have been*, but that isn't considered a major issue — and rightly! The main point is that he was caught up in the group aura of that dancing, chanting, music-making procession as it came down from the sacred hill, and he was moved to shout or sing prophetic utterances aloud, as the rest were doing. To people who knew Saul, this in itself evidently caused astonishment.

Telepathy can be, and often is, involved in some types of prediction.

This is particularly the case when someone seeks a forecast on the outcome of what should really be a personal decison.

The unconscious mind of the questioner frequently KNOWS the answer to a problem of this sort, but is not allowed to transmit its knowledge into consciousness because an emotional reaction, perhaps of guilt or fear, blocks the way. Help is therefore needed, to bring the unconscious decision into consciousness.

Another interesting form of telepathy sometimes makes its appearance, in which a psychic link exists between two people (relatives usually), but owing to their lack of developed awareness this link remains lost in unconsciousness. Then one of them comes in contact with a person who, whether by training or any other

cause, has a more acute perception. *and the percip-
ient can read, through the unconscious mind of the
person there present, matters of which that person
is unaware concerning the absent one.*

Thus, in the biblical story to which we have referred, almost the first thing Samuel says to Saul is that
the animals he had been seeking were safely found; as
we learn, they had been returned to Saul's father.

There is also the type of happening which is attributed to *instinct*. Instinct, in whatever species, is as
varied in its manifestations as are the life functions it
prompts or protects: despite research, its mode of action sometimes remains enigmatic.

Even when we think we have a piece of instinctual
behavior charted, a change due to changed circumstances can highlight our failure to pinpoint its underlying causes. We know, for example, of the instinctual
behavior of salmon in returning from the ocean to breed
in the same river where they themselves were bred. For
many years in different parts of the world salmon have
been marked and observed, and the verdict was unan-
imous. There was no margin of hazard or error; salmon
don't vary or make mistakes. So we could only assume
this was a fixed, mechanical thing; the salmon were just
"programmed" for the one river they were hatched in.

Following the 1980 eruption of Mount St. Helens,
when two notable salmon rivers, the Cowlitz and
Toutle, were choked with debris, it seemed evident that
the fish returning to those rivers from the ocean would,

literally, be heading for disaster. The big twenty-to-thirty pounders were expected to die in a compulsive attempt to mount the impassable rivers.

The fish made no such attempt; instead, they all swam up the nearby Kalama. *We, as human beings, don't expect much guidance from this kind of instinct; but we have our own collective levels, whose influence over many people is visibly increased in emergencies.*

Coming back to the subject of prediction, there are always some predictions which, no matter how carefully we analyze the circumstances, are not clearly explainable. We can consider for instance the various predictions of airplane crashes, railroad crashes, accidents generally. (We leave earthquakes and volcanic eruptions out of it because these certainly are heralded by subtle vibrations and pressures on the material level which can be felt and identified by some highly sensitive people before even the most delicate instrument could do so.) It has been shown repeatedly that before an air or rail disaster there are frequently people who "know" danger lies ahead, or who just "on impulse" change their bookings. How does this work?

We can't assume, for instance, that there is *in every case* something in the unconscious mind of a pilot or signalman or other operator, which knows a circuit or engine will fail, or he himself have a blackout or heart attack, during the journey. In some cases, certainly, there MAY BE subliminal perceptions—and telepathic reception of these—regarding some slightly irregular sound in an engine, or some ignored malaise in a human body. In other cases, however, there is no possibility of such communication, and a person has only an unexplained consciousness that a rock or a machine or some kind of non-living structure "feels" dangerous. This may be due in some cases to a hint from the Collective Unconscious, or an astral exploration; but the likeliest cause is a warning auric vibration.

Sources of Prophecy

It is evident, then, that material which appears in a prophetic utterance is likely to come from a variety of sources. (As a preliminary, all the norms, facts or traditions which are accepted by the seer have to be recognized. Even these, however, usually pass through the unconscious mind of the seer before being incorporated into prophetic material; we frequently find that no matter how recognizable their source may be, they are in some way transformed, as, for instance, modified to accomodate a symbolic value.)

The main sources from which prophetic material is drawn can be indicated as follows:

1.   *Intimations from the Higher Self, conveyed to an evolved and receptive mental level of the seer's psyche. (This high matter is, strictly, beyond the scope of this book but needs to be recognized.)*
2.   *Material drawn by telepathy from the minds of others; knowledge of their intentions, attitudes, etc.*

This can include much of which the other parties are unaware, including purposes they have not yet recognized, and rational deductions they may have repressed as being unwelcome.

3.   Rational deductions of the seer's own which have passed into the unconscious because of emotional connotations.

4.   Material gathered by the sensitive aura, and passed into the unconscious mind until either need or opportunity brings it forth. This can include physical facts of the present or of the past, and emotional states of other people.

5.   Astral material gathered by the emotional and instinctual nature of the seer in its own right as a native of the astral world. This can be (a) material proper to the astral world itself, including "the shape of things to come", and (b) material gathered by the astral body — or by a part of its substance reconnoitering in the physical world.

6.   Spiritually, mentally or emotionally perceived implications of facts observed in the physical world (e.g., climatic signs, political trends, the public temper, or the behavior of an individual.)

7.   Material received from the Collective Unconscious. This is likely, because of the archetypal images, to introduce echoes of religious or folk traditions, but the main connotations will be universal in nature.

8.   There is the possibility of gaining knowledge from several different sources, and unconsciously working up

these perhaps fragmentary facts so as to make a coherent whole. *Error can creep in here, particularly where there has been a bias in the preliminary selection of facts; but the unconscious mind is generally quite an expert Sherlock Holmes!*

If you wish to cultivate your aptitude for prophecy, you can very well leave most of these complicated "mechanisms" to your unconscious mind, which after all is well equipped by nature to deal with them. *But you have to encourage your unconscious mind by giving it opportunites to develop its powers.*

That psyche—YOUR PSYCHE— which is growing in awareness of its potential, becomes capable of self-realization at progressively more profound levels than those known to everyday consciousness: it needs but congenial circumstances for the hidden levels to rise to the surface and manifest their intrinsic qualities. *As you grow in experience of the life-style indicated in the previous three chapters, as you strengthen your relationship with the life-force at all levels, the deeper realities which transcend temporal and spatial co-ordinates will come readily closer to your consciousness.*

We shall presently be giving a method of developing the art of *scrying*, an important way by which the faculty of foreknowledge can be nurtured; for it is one of the ways in which you learn to accept impressions, vibrations, perceptions, certainties which come to you through the unconscious levels of YOUR OWN PSYCHE instead of through the physical senses or by means of rational deduction. Meantime, we give some simple practices for group use, by which from time to time the faculties of prediction and of "reading" material which has been physically seen by another can be tested; with, also, a fun game to develop those same faculties.

Finding Out

Using the ESP cards in group activity is a good way to *find out* if you and your friends have special prophetic aptitudes, or how these are developing. Everyone can OCCASIONALLY run through a "cards unseen" routine, the results being examined not only for direct better-than-20% scores, but also for any evidence of time-slip in the results.

As progress is made, you should sometimes have *a test on prediction specifically*. This is distinguished by the person to be tested declaring, just before the test, that *the card to be named will not be the one the operator has just put up, but the one the operator is going to put up next*. This declaration will be made aloud and with deliberation, so that both the conscious and unconscious mind will accept it. The test then proceeds and is recorded in the same way as a normal "cards unseen" test, though it should be noted on the head of the card as prediction test; the results can be expected to show a higher "forecast" score than is reached by the same person in other tests where prediction is accidental.

An interesting little operation, which tests for the ability to pull facts out of the operator's *subliminal awareness* can be organized thus:

Whoever is acting as operator shuffles the ESP cards, then quietly and reflectively goes through them, looking attentively at the symbol on each one in turn and stacking the seen cards carefully in their initial order. When the twenty-five have been looked at in this way, the deck is put aside in a closed box.

Next day, or rather later, when the operator is certainly unable to call consciously to mind the sequence of the cards, other members of the group are asked to list it out by psychic inspiration. Finally, each person's list is compared with the contents of the box. *If the results are better than their "cards unseen" scores,* we can reasonably assume the operator's subliminal memory has caused the difference. (This practice is most effective if the operator prepares it without the group's knowledge, then confronts them with the box and asks them to list the cards in it.)

Call-in

(This game with ESP cards is good for everyone's development in prediction and telepathy.)

For 2 to 5 players, one 25-card deck of ESP cards is needed. For more than 5 players, two identical decks should be used.)

Three cards are dealt to each player, and the remaining cards (the "stack") are placed face down near the center of the table.

To illustrate play, let us say there are three players, "A", "B", and "C".

To commence, "A" takes a card from the top of the stack, looks at it, then places it face down in the center of the table. *(This is one of the few times when a player looks at a card just taken from the stack.)*

"B" has to guess this card. He names it aloud, then turns it face up. If he was right, he takes that card into his hand. In that case, "A" takes the next card from the top of the stack *(without looking at it)* and places it, still face down, in the center. "B" has to guess that too, and, if successful, takes it.

"A" deals the next card from the top of the stack into center, and so the procedure continues until "B" turns over a card and is seen to have guessed wrong. When this happens, the card "B" guessed wrongly is put at random into the stack, which can if desired be re-shuffled and cut at this point. "B" then places any one card from his hand, face down, in the center and "C" has to guess it. If right, "C" takes that card into his hand and "B" deals the next card from the top of the stack for "C" to guess. If "C" is wrong, the card he is wrong on is placed at random in the stack (which again can be re-shuffled and cut at this point) and "C" then chooses any one card from his hand and places it in the center for "A" to guess.

Each player thus begins his guesses, in each round of the game, with a card already seen by his neighbor; if he gets that one right, he proceeds to cards which have not been seen by any player.

Each player drops out of the game if, having no cards in his hand, *he is required to deal a card into the center and is unable to do so*. Merely having no cards isn't in itself sufficient reason to drop out; two or three right guesses could put the player "back in business". *A player who drops out takes a card from the stack, looks at it and places it, as at start of play.*

The game ends when all players but one have had to drop out, or when only one card is left in the stack. In that case, players can be awarded points according to the number of cards they are holding.

———————————

We come now to consider the practice of Scrying, one of the traditional modes in which material from the deeper levels of the psyche can be drawn into consciousness.

The material you obtain by your use of this method may come from any of the sources we have previously indicated. At first it will probably be limited to past or present happenings or circumstances; however, as you become more experienced and your conscious mind more readily accepts what flows to it from the wellspring of the unconscious, intimations of future happenings and circumstances will come to be included.

Vision Mirror
1. Initial Practice for individuals

This is designed to "open" the faculty for you; that is, to give you access to images, ideas, feelings—any or all of these according to your individual temperament—from your unconscious mind. You should perform it alone, no matter whether you are a member of a group or will be continuing solo. A suggestion for group fun will follow, *but individual proficiency must be achieved first.*

The time you take for a scrying session can vary from forty minutes (minimum) to two hours (maximum) according to your needs, your inclination and the exigencies of your time-table. You should maintain enthusiasm and regular practice; but scrying is in all its forms a fascinating art, and is not difficult if you set out with a clear idea of what to expect.

The Vision Mirror — like any other scrying instrument — is designed for "visual" use, in the sense that the scryer's gaze is to rest upon it. *But this does not mean your eyes are going to perceive pictures in the Mirror,* although many scryers do experience an impression that this happens. If you see pictures, it will be with your "mind's eye", it will not be with your physical eyes, no matter how clear the pictures appear; they may seem to be "in the Mirror", or you may be aware of them in your imagination as if you ought to be seeing them in the Mirror. And if, instead or besides, you receive a stream of ideas or of emotions or of "hunches" — convictions, based on reasons unknown to you, that certain matters *are so*—these are from the same source as the images and are totally as valid.

Place your Vision Mirror, with its back to the light, on a table covered with a dark—preferably black—cloth, and put a chair in front of it so that when you sit here you will be two or three feet from the mirror. Arrange the height of the mirror so that while seated you can look directly into its center without inclining your head or eyes noticeably up or down.

To begin your session, it is a good thing to stand facing the Mirror and to utter an earnest aspiration *to find and to control the powers of knowledge and vision which are in your psyche.* Put this in whatever words come naturally to you, *but speak them aloud,* dwell on their meaning and become thoroughly attuned to them.

Seat youself before the Mirror in a balanced, easy pose. Rest your gaze on the center of the Mirror; any time you find your eyes straying off center, simply bring them back. Let your mind wander as it will, in a meditative, dreamy way, avoiding subjects of intellectual or emotional tension. Remain conscious of the Mirror; don't concern yourself with anything else.

In the early stages optical illusions may appear, but these should not be encouraged. They are no aid to true seership; although the mode of perceiving images in scrying differs, as we have said, from person to person, it is in any case different in nature from the mode of seeing physical illusions.

When true images or impressions "appear," in whatever mode this happens to you, *you will know*. It is a definite release within you of a source not before accessible to you in this way. You are "dreaming awake." There is a sense of inebriation, which some describe as "Riding a wave."

In this early practice in scrying, your purpose is to receive images or impressions as clearly and steadily as you can. You are not seeking to "interpret" anything, but to receive it clearly and to understand what it is in itself. If anything is unclear, *ask a question about it, aloud, and wait for the point to be made plain.*

This clarity can be achieved as surely if you possess the more "abstract" type of perception as with the more visual, and in either case it is worth your while to be particular about it from the early stages.

When the flow of images or impressions customarily begins early in your scrying sessions, and you can soon render these distinct and clear if they are not so at the outset, then you are ready to proceed to the next stage: you have "opened the faculty."

2. Second-stage Practice for Individuals
Answering Questions by Scrying.

In this second stage, having successfully opened the faculty, you are ready to learn to change, direct and control the images you see, or the impressions you receive, so as to obtain answers to your questions .

For this purpose, plan your main questions and lines of inquiry in advance, so as not to be cogitating these matters during the scrying session itself.

Frame your opening aspiration to state plainly and briefly your intention to gain certain knowledge by scrying, specifying the subject.

When seated in front of your Vision Mirror, relax your mind and ask your first question: then wait passively for the response. When an image, thought or feeling manifests itself, consider what bearing it has upon the subject of your question, and formulate your next question accordingly.

If an image, idea or feeling appears which has no relevance to your question, *you should repeat the question in new and very exact terms.* Even if a response, or a valid response, is long delayed, *you should not give up.* The truth of whatever you seek CAN BE HAD, and since you seek it you should persevere.

Bear in mind that when the answer comes it may not be during your Vision Mirror sessions. Not infrequently a delayed answer, or a clue to it, will appear in your dreams.

If you have a dream which seems related to the matter of your question but which still doesn't give a clear enough or full enough answer, *ask further about it in your next scrying session.* You are dealing with the same levels of your psyche, by whichever means you are in communication with them.

When the material which rises into your consciousness is unimpeded by your successive questions, remains lucid and forceful and readily takes on the direction of your inquiry, you can consider you are truly developing the faculty of scrying. The length of time taken to achieve this cannot be predetermined; it depends entirely on the individual. Continue your practice alone while you are exploring your potential; you should feel completely familiar with this and at ease in it before going on to group work in scrying.

Keep records of all your scrying sessions. Write down what you have seen, as soon as you can afterwards. Even right at the beginning when what you see may be only one simple image, make a note of it. If you see matters which are completely meaningless to you, write them too. Some of them may one day make good sense to you. At all events, your scrying sessions are an important chapter of your inner life.

3. Scrying in Group

This is, in its effect, one of the lighter group activities, but it presupposes that the scryer's "homework" has been faithfully done! It is given in outline here; you and your group can arrange details.

At any session for this game, *only one person will scry:* all group members are invited to be present, and the more there are the more fun there will be.

The Vision Mirror—preferably the scryer's own—

is set up as previously described. The scryer having left the room, a chosen member of the group sits before the Mirror and, looking into the Mirror for a full five minutes, allows the mind to be occupied with anything he or she wishes — meditation, daydreaming, silently reciting a poem, whatever. When the time has expired, the "sitter" rejoins the company and the scryer is recalled by a signal.

The scryer now takes the chair, after making an initial aspiration which includes the intention of discovering the sitter's identity. During the scrying session which follows, the scryer's objective is to build up a recognizable portrait of the sitter, in terms of personality, circumstances and activities. To this end, the scryer will not only speak aloud any guiding questions as when scrying in solitude, but also should utter, to whatever extent he or she may feel moved to do so, the content of the flow from the unconscious. Material for this will mostly be drawn from past and present, but with a good session and a true perception of the sitter, the door of foreknowledge can be opened too.

Everyone else who is present should however keep silence until the scrying is ended.

SCRYING RECORD

Name _____ Date _____

Instrument _____ Time start ____ end ____
If part of
a series, No. _____ Moon Phase ____ Sign ____

Question, if any _____

_____

Notes of Images sensed:

Other Questions:

Conclusions:

Any later dreams felt to relate to this session:

Checkpoint

4

- Essentials to developing your power to predict:
  - (a) Keeping up your meditation practices.
  - (b) Keeping up your contacts: with the natural world, with the human world, and with your Higher Self.
  - (c) Spending time with people who already have prophetic powers, or at least with others who seek those powers. This will not only benefit you psychically — it will help you find your tongue!

- Prophecy is frequently a matter of telling people things which only an emotional barrier prevents them from knowing consciously themselves.

- You may find prediction material comes to your

mind, not connected with the person you are talking to but with someone else who is known to that person.

- *Study often* the list of sources of Prophecy on pages 101–103. It will give you much insight into ways in which different functions of the psyche work together in unity.

- With ESP cards—
  (a) Test "Cards Unseen" in the usual way, and scan the results for "time-slip".
  (b) Test "Cards Unseen" with a declared intention of naming, each time, the card which will be put up next.
  (c) Do the telepathy test on page 105.

- Play "Call-in," an exciting game to develop both telepathy and prediction!

- Practice with your Vision Mirror as described in this chapter, to develop insights into past, present and future.

- Watch your dreams for delayed answers to questions you ask in scrying.

- "Scrying in Group"—a great test for the competent scryer, and good fun too for all present.

Study Points

5

1. Psychometry: the psychic sensing, through touch, of the circumstances associated with a material object:

   a. Circumstances related to the object itself.

   b. Particulars about persons who have previously touched the object.

2. Every object, like every living being, has an astral level, which is extremely susceptible to impressions.

   a. The more forceful the impression, i.e., the more the emotional force, the visual imagery, etc., the more easily sensed it will be.

   b. The auric energy of the possessor of an object impinges upon its astral level, leaving an impression representative of that person—his life, feelings, experiences, etc.

    c. Even the object's own history—its origins or formation—can be read at the appropriate astral level.

    d. The innate "character" of the object, or of its composition, can be read and related in terms of its magical or planetary attributions.

3. Generally speaking, more recent impressions associated with an object will be read first—but it is also true that a more powerful impression, even if earlier, can take precedence over a later, weaker one.

4. In a state of calm relaxation, allow your consciousness to receive material which your emotional-instinctual nature will transmit, *through your unconscious mind,* from the astral vibrations of the object being held or touched.

    a. Study the image of the Lily Pond given in this chapter as analogous to the process of impressions arising from the depths of the unconscious to the surface of consciousness.

5

Astral Imprints

We have mentioned in chapter 3 the faculty shown by some rare people of using the physical sense of touch in unusual ways, to perceive color or flavor. (As a fact, flavor is always perceived by contact: normally, between the hightly sensitized skin surfaces meeting in mouth or throat, but in these off-beat cases it can be by bringing together the fingers with moist salt or icing sugar, for instance, on the delicate skin between them.

These unorthdox faculties are not unduly surprising; for, just as the outer regions of head and face are almost totally conditioned to sense-perception in its five modes, so the hands too are powerfully associated with similar perceptiveness in more adventurous form: feeling, trying and testing. *Nor can we suppose this association to be limited to the physical body, since its impulses derive from the psyche.*

There is, indeed, a truly psychic ability to be developed from using the sense of touch: the handling of material objects so as to become aware of circumstances relating to them, or to bring into consciousness particulars about persons who have previously touched them, in the art of PSYCHOMETRY.

Here we are usually concerned with impressions which have been transferred to these objects by the activity of people's emotional—instinctual nature, without any deliberate intention. At this point it will be useful, however, for a clearer understanding of what really takes place, to bring in a passage from *The Secrets of Dr. Taverner* in which Dion Fortune says something about an occult technique for PURPOSELY imbuing a thing with a psychic impression.

In the history of "The Scented Poppies" we have a discussion concerning a moonstone. This stone, or others similar, had been introduced into the homes of several people without their knowledge, along with some seeds containing a certain drug; and those people proceeded, apparently without motive, to take their own lives. Taverner finds this stone, and is giving his friends an idea of how the impulse to suicide has been impressed upon it; but in accordance with occult tradition in those stricter times, he is far from specific.

" 'The moonstone is turned to a keynote, and that keynote is suicide,' said Taverner. 'Someone . . . has impressed that picture (I won't tell you how) on that moonstone, so that anyone who is in close contact with it finds the same image rise into his mind, just as a depressed person can infect others with depression without speaking one single word to them.' " There follows some debate on various modes of existence of *mind*, in terms strongly derived from Rosicrucian teachings and with particular reference to crystalline stones, but the main point is left in very general terms:

" 'Then,' said Polson, 'you think someone has imprinted an idea on the soul of that moonstone so that anyone who was sensitive would be influenced by it, and then added the seeds . . . to drug an ordinary person into abnormal sensitiveness . . . ?' "

" 'Exactly!' "

What is disguised, or put roundabout, in Taverner's (and Dion Fortune's) account of the matter, is the connecting link of the astral world. What Polson calls "the soul" of the moonstone is the astral level of its existence. And astral existence generally, including the astral level of any living being or inanimate object, is highly susceptible to impressions, and forceful impressions especially, which meet it in its own domain. It follows that for an operation of the kind which is in question here, there must have been built up a strong emotional force, doubtless including also some powerful visual imagery, and this force must by occult means have been "driven" into the astral substance of the stone.

It is upon the *astral level* of any object, then, that

influences can be impressed whether knowingly or
unknowingly. The auric energy of the possessor of the
object, in particular, inevitably impinges upon that
astral level, and when intense or long-continued emotions are present the effect will be proportionately
powerful. Even a general atmosphere, such as of a war
or a natural cataclysm, can be registered by the astral
level of an object.

The total of influences carried by an object may,
however, be immense.

Let us consider as an example another gemstone;
not one, like the Moonstone, which has been deliberately impressed with a psychic communication, but one
which since being mounted as a piece of jewelry has
passed, maybe, through the hands of several possessors
and has been worn on many uneventful occasions as
well as a few critical ones.

You might in certain circumstances receive a
panoramic view of all that. Or you might — but this
would be very advanced psychometry — get behind all
that to the making of the stone itself: its volcanic or
meteoric origin in vast fires when no life was yet present,
and the long ages of slow cooling and pressure in the
earth's crust. Or you might receive something of the
drama and fascination of the gemstone market, the
deliberation of the lapidary over the stone's form and
structure, its cutting and setting.

Another aspect of the stone's existence which you

might receive is the concourse of its own influences as *itself*, a particular stone of a particular kind; the vibrations of the sort which have led some gems to be attributed through the ages to Jupiter, some to Venus or the Sun, or to the other planetary spheres. The color, brilliance and innate "character" of diamond, ruby, zircon, opal and the rest are involved at a deep level with these attributions.

Generally speaking, with any object which you psychometrize, more recent impressions associated with it will come to you more readily than earlier ones. There are exceptions, however.

A powerful earlier impression can take precedence over a weaker later one. Besides this, *earlier impressions can be reinforced by repetition.*

These last two considerations come into play in what is sometimes described as the "haunting" of certain objects. For instance, over a period of years, a succession of people who fall asleep in a particular armchair, all dream the same thing. *Nobody ever seems to dream of the succession of people falling asleep in that chair;* the earlier incident, whatever it may be, takes precedence. In addition to the initial force of the incident, it can also gain impetus as more people envision it.

Using Psychometry

There are some important resemblances between

psychometry and scrying; there are also great differences. During psychometry you are working with the astral vibrations of the object you psychometrize. It is held in your hands, and while you are psychometrizing it you cradle it, pass it from one hand to the other, and from time to time turn it about; this contact aids your awareness of the object, besides helping to settle your mind into tranquility.

In a state of calm relaxation, allow your reflective faculties to function, unimpeded by analytical processes, so that your consciousness is free to receive the material which your emotional—instinctual nature will transmit to it from the astral vibrations of the object being psychometrized.

As the flow of material from the unconscious increases, your consciousness should receive it altogether passively. Let the object "talk" while you "listen." You are "dreaming awake" while the rising psychic material takes its own course, progressively unfolding.

The process of psychometry has been likened to the growing of water-lilies. The concept is of a lake, whose serene and placid water represents the mind; the lilies represent material gathered in psychometry, which arises from the deeps to blossom in consciousness.

As in scrying, the material which reaches your consciousness may present itself to you in various forms: as mental imagery, or as ideas or feelings.

You should always verbalize the material which comes to your consciousness; this is good procedure in psychometry, even when you are alone. *Unlike the process in scrying, however, you do not in psychometry utter, or even think, directing questions, nor try to guide the development of new material from that which you have received.* The deeper faculties of your unconscious mind will from time to time work together in the interpretation of the vibrations; and that which arises from them into your consciousness will contain greater truth than the object and its immediate associations might seem capable of yielding.

As you progress further in the practice of psychometry, your conscious mind will become more proficient in transmitting the astral material, proportionately as you give more heed to it. You, too, as a person, will become more skilled in psychometry as you gain more practice in it.

Pointers for Practice

1.   You should, initially, practice psychometry *alone,* free from any distraction. Have a tape-recorder in action for these sessions; not only will you then have a record of your utterances for later reference, but, more important, it will relieve your mind of the possible stress and concern of trying to remember the material you receive.

2.   In developing the faculty, you should use items which will give you opportunities to explore a variety of different types of astral vibration, in order to gain experience of their distinctive "feel."

A good procedure is to psychometrize, on different occasions, items with certain features in common and certain contrasted differences, so that you may gain ability and confidence in discerning the vibrations involved in each case. You could for example buy a sec-one-hand prayer-book and psychometrize it, then an old well-thumbed novel; or you could acquire an old piece of jewelry and a newly-tumbled gemstone, or an old and a new piece of craftwork.

Don't rush this collecting and psychometrizing of different materials; it is a fascinating and rewarding phase of your self-training. When, however, you feel you have developed real confidence in you abilities, you can proceed to work at psychometry with members of your group.

3.   In a group whose members are practicing psychometry, opportunities occur when objects can be psychometrized, whose history and associations are verifiable. On occasions when a person is psychometrizing for the group (and it is advisable that in no one session should more than one person psychometrize), the articles which other members bring along for psychometry may be their own property or may come from close friends or relatives; in all cases they should be brought along wrapped in several thicknesses of clean paper *(not news-print)* or polythene, to be unwrapped at the moment of handing to the psychometrist.

On these occasions, discussion or verification of material given by the psychometrist should be reserved for the last part of the meeting, when no more psy-chometry is being done.

The more-than-physical contacts of psychometry can reveal a fuller meaning in many experiences which, in everyday speech, are usually expressed already in terms of "touch." We may, for instance, acquire an object which has belonged to someone unknown to us, and we can be "touched" by that person's emotions. By holding a keepsake we can truly "keep in touch" with an absent friend. People who live in artificial conditions find their collection of rocks, or their plants, prevent their "losing touch" with the natural world, and we can deeply share that experience. Or we may have a real "touchstone," in more than the popular sense of that word, if we possess some object whose associations will renew, when we hold it, our inner loyalties and an awareness of our ideals. Psychometry is far more than an "interesting" faculty: it is a conscious perception of the inter-relatedness of life's currents.

The Lily Pond

Checkpoint
5

- Psychometry is the art of bringing into your consciousness any knowledge or emotional impressions whose vibrations your unconscious mind "picks up" from the astral substance of a material object. Some of these vibrations come from the object itself, but the vibrations of human emotions become imprinted in the astral substance of articles much worn or handled, and these vibrations are generally the easiest to "pick up."

- As a general rule, when you psychometrize an object you will receive its more recent impressions more readily than its earlier ones. But a powerful earlier impression can come to you more readily than a weaker later one; also, earlier impressions can be intensified through repetition.

- Psychometry is performed by holding the object which is to be psychometrized, and stilling the "outer" and more analytical levels of your psyche so that impressions received by its emotional— instinctual level can rise unimpeded into your consciousness.

  Let the object "talk" while you "listen". While you psychometrize, you are "dreaming awake."

  Remember the lily pond! The water, serene and placid, is your mind. The lily plant grows from the deeps, through the water to blossom at the surface—that is, in your consciousness.

- Speak aloud the images, ideas, feeling which come to you in psychometry, and have a recorder taping your practice sessions. That will preserve your utterances and will obviate any need for you to try to remember what comes to you.

- Practice alone until you have full confidence in your abilities, then go on to group psychometry.

- Obtain items both old and new for the purpose of psychometrizing them, and learn to distinguish their different types of influence.

- Objects intended for psychometry should be kept

carefully wrapped until the time comes for them to be examined. *Make this a custom always.*

- Reserve any discussion of matters which come up in group psychometry until the end of the session.

- Don't forget your meditations and other good practices! They will all aid in psychometry by keeping the different levels of your psyche harmonious, sensitive and inter-related.

Study Points

6

1. Just as joining forces with a group of like-minded people is a way for you to gain help in your own psychic development program, so you may also be able to gain help from "discarnate" beings.

2. If you do undertake a spiritualist program for development with the members of your own group forming a "circle," you should open every "sitting" with the Tabor Formulation as previously established for your group meetings. After this, the leader of the circle utters on behalf of all some words of aspiration, and an invocation of divine blessing on the circle.

   a. The spiritualist approach is just a part of your basic psychic development program, and therefore you should continue with your testing, game—playing, dietary considerations, exercises, etc.

b. During your "sittings" you may be given advice on matters relating to your program, but you must remember that it is for you to decide, or for the group's leader to decide, what action if any will be taken.

3. Trance: Light Trance is achieved collectively in the circle when all participants sit breathing gently and evenly, with the mind becoming relaxed and stilled, opening the way for the Unconscious Mind through which any communications must come.
   a. The group leader, however, must not go into trance: he is to remain in "control."
   b. Deep Trance may occur with a genuine contact, but no one should TRY to go into deep trance.

4. A "Guide" is a body-guard to a particular person or to the circle as a whole—ensuring that no one suffers physical or psychic harm.

5. Energy must be made available for the spirit entities to manifest:
   a. The linking of hands by members of the circle increases the circulation of energy, and can be undertaken at any time a need for extra energy seems desirable.
   b. Incense also increases the circulation of energy,

and also acts as a "signal" that your sitting is taking place.

c. Music, either live or recorded, and song will also liberate energy, and help induce and maintain harmony in the circle.

d. A red light is also useful in stirring up energy and in aiding astral sight.

6. Problems in sittings are easily met by exercising authority—remembering it is the *incarnate* humans who are "running the show"—and any unwelcome elemental, or disturbing entity should be ordered out of the circle.

   a. Your guide, or guides, can be called upon for help, and should be requested not to let the problem occur again.

6

The Spiritualist

Approach*

All the major religions and the esoteric traditions of the world affirm, in varying modes and degrees, the simple fact of human survival after death. For the *intervention* of discarnate beings in the lives of the incarnate, on occasion, let us say at once there is evidence; and a small proportion of very strong evidence.

Evidence, not proof. Proof is, at our current state of knowledge, impossible.

The reason for this impossibility of proof is that still, despite much research in many lands, we have no ideas of the limits of what is possible for an *incarnate* human being, consciously and unconsciously, to do.

---

* To use one's psychism in a spiritualist, way must be an entirely personal decision. Those who either do not wish to do so or do not feel they are ready for it can proceed to Chapter 7 without detriment to their psychic development program.

In fact, with more research we seem to see the solution to the mystery receding ever further from us, as the resources of our unconscious are explored and are found to be greater, vaster, than were ever supposed. At what phenomenon dare we stop and say the psyche of a living person COULD NOT in any circumstances, normal or abnormal, have caused it?

An old but well-received history of a psychic occurrence in Britain will serve as example; it concerns a lady whose deceased brother appeared to her one night. The background to this event is that both of them had been skeptics in matters of religion, but had made a pact of a usual type, that the first one to leave this world would return to let the other one know the truth of the matter. On the night in question, the apparition pronounced completely in favor of the Christian revelation. The lady not only remained skeptical, but added that in the morning she would probably feel sure she'd dreamed the whole happening.

The apparition countered this objection by pulling the whole width of a heavy curtain through one of its suspension rings: a feat the lady admitted she couldn't normally perform. *"But I might have such strength if I were sleep-walking,"* she pointed out; in response to which, the apparition touched her wrist and vanished. When she awoke in the morning, the lady found there was a patch of withered tissue in her wrist, which remained all her life; and this was taken as conclusive, both for the objective reality of the apparition and for the authority of its message.

But why?

To begin with, it should be seen clearly that no opinion concerning the nature or the objective reality of this apparition can have any bearing, one way or the other, upon the question of the Christian religion.

Religions are neither *proved* nor *disproved* in that kind of way, whether we are talking about Christianity or Spiritualism or any other human belief. Alike in true manifestations of the departed (when these occur) and in material unconsciously "projected" from the psyche of an incarnate person, there is too great an overplus of the emotional, image-making level of the psyche for spiritual reality to gain any clear evidence from their testimony.

That, therefore, is not what is in question here.

The question is, why someone who is willing to grant that an incarnate person in an altered state of consciousness (like sleepwalking) might be able to put forth abnormal strength, should yet be unable to suppose that in the same or another state of consciousness lasting scars could be produced upon the physical body?

The answer may be that our modern knowledge of physical effects produced by mind-power was necessary before anyone could accept this possibility.

Another point we have to consider, as researchers,

is this: IF the lady's unconscious mind was trying to convince her of something (that is one of the possibilities) then it *had to* set up a "block" at some point to prevent her continuing to see flaws in its argument. *This is a hazard every single one of us is liable to in one form or another,* and a great advantage of group activity is to keep our inquiries from being dominated by some unconscious individual bias.

Powers of the Incarnate

In the preceding chapters we've seen some of the things you as an incarnate human being can do:

YOU CAN learn to start, stop, or change the direction of the swing of a pendulum when neither you nor any other person is touching it or its cord.

YOU CAN use your pendulum, again, to discover facts which are unknown to your conscious mind.

YOU CAN also practice divination by the use of a Vision Mirror, and by calling "unseen" dice, and by calling cards, some of which have been seen, some not.

YOU CAN by contact with a material object, enter into the emotions and experiences of its owner.

YOU CAN also practice predicting the future, and allied arts of seership—telling people things which maybe have already happened but neither they nor you knew, and things they've forgotten.

All these things you know YOU CAN DO, because EVERYBODY can who gives them their interest, practice and patience and who builds their life along natural healthful lines as we've indicated. *Further psychic powers you can develop, and insights into how such powers work, will be given in the course of this book.*

But do you always gather your extra-sensory knowledge, or practice your psychic abilities, *unaided?*

As you've already seen, you certainly need not! Joining forces with a group of like-minded people is a way to more available energy and ease of action for everyone concerned.

But what about discarnate help?

It's possible we all receive much more of this than we realize, and can do more in return to help the discarnate ones with *their* projects. That is the spiritualist position. Once again, it means a pooling of energies, a sharing of understanding and resources for easier and more effective action.

This is no "short cut;" it remains that the person who has taken time and trouble to develop his or her other psychic faculties, and a potent lifestyle, will be far more effective than the one who only sits passively waiting to be used as "an instrument".

A SHARP KNIFE AND A BLUNT ONE ARE BOTH "INSTRUMENTS," BUT WHICH ONE WOULD YOU USE?

Whether the spiritualist way of using psychism is "right" for you, is an entirely personal decision.

If you and your group are interested in trying some practical work along spiritualist lines, you can look

forward to experiences which will enrich your understanding of general psychic practices, just as your general psychic practices will help you in this.

It's best at first not to philosophize too much
about results; that can come later, when you have some
experience of what the results are like. Later in this
chapter we shall look at some different angles on
the matter, but the best initial attitude is to be quite
unbiased and take each experience as it comes.

We are reminded of an old comment by G.K.
Chesterton, to the effect that the man who is taken
in by life is anyway better off than the man who is
thrown out by life. In other words, the gold in them
thar hills may be "fool's gold," but if anyone tells you
so before you get there, thank him kindly for his counsel and go get you own sample for testing just the same.

The Sitting

When you meet for a spiritualist sitting, however
experimental, it should be understood that it isn't much
use giving this activity less than an hour—two hours are
better—and quite a lot of the time will be spent sitting
in a circle which should not be broken. If, while you are
all beginners, the first hour passes with "nothing happening," at the end of that time the leader of the circle
could review the postion and see if enough people wish
to go on through the second hour, but nothing less
than the whole of the first hour can be considered a
fair test.

Settle everyone on comfortable chairs placed in a circle, and have the circle the right size so each individual can hold hands with the people to right and left. If you have enough people to form two concentric circles, that's fine. If you have fewer people than that, but more than you can place in a circle to fit the room, let the extra people sit behind the ones in the circle. (The "circle" can be an ellipse, of course!)

When hands are linked, each person at the back can place a hand upon the shoulder of a person in the circle. Or the back row can sit near each other and link hands with each other; then the person at the left-hand end of the back row will place his or her left hand on the shoulder of a person in front, while the person at the right-hand end of the back row will do the same with his or her right hand. Nobody, during the progress of the circle, should sit with arms or legs crossed. Hands, when not linked, should rest upon the thighs.

It is usual in Spiritualist meetings to open the circle with the linking of hands and prayer, to unify and energize the circle.

Your members, naturally, will open the sessions with the potent Tabor Formulation. After this, the leader of the circle utters on behalf of the group, in whatever words he feels inspired to use, an aspiration to achieve true, beneficent and illuminating contact with those who have passed from this world into the realms of spirit; he then invokes divine blessing and protection on the members of the circle.

Trance

Trance of some degree is an almost constant condition of spirit communication. Should you develop a capacity for deep trance, you have to accept the fact that you may know nothing of your best achievements as a *trance medium,* except what other people tell you or what may be recorded on tape.

There are degrees of trance, just as there are of hypnosis. A light trance state is not initially very distinguishable from the "normal" state, either to the observer or to the person experiencing it; but the attention is *more* open to non-material influences, and correspondingly *less* to earthly happenings, while insight and comprehension are progressively sharpened.

This is achieved collectively in circle, when all sit breathing gently and evenly, with the mind wandering as it will and becoming relaxed and gently stilled into a state very similar to that of falling asleep. Each person knows that sufficient alertness must be maintained to pay attention if anything is said by the leader of the circle; but a hypnagogic condition is nevertheless reached, where inconsequent ideas and words flash vividly from time to time through the consciousness. The atmosphere of the circle, the group's psychic unity, and the acknowledged purpose of the sitting, are all signals to the unconscious mind that the essential action is to take place in its domain; and all assist to transform the state of suspended thought into true light trance, into subtle other-worldly awareness.

(It should be understood by everyone in the circle that no matter what may befall, the leader of the circle does not go into trance.)

Anyone in the circle who has reached the light trance state described above, and who feels impelled to speak, should do so no matter how "foolish" the matter may seem, or how convinced the speaker may feel that the words come only from his or her own unconscious mind. Any communication must in any case come through the unconscious mind; there may indeed be a genuine contact with a spirit being, and if there is, utterance will increase the current of communication. There should be no attempt made to go into a state of deep trance; if a contact has been made, this may become strengthened to a point at which deep trance may supervene spontaneously.

Visitors, Guides and Controls

Some of your spirit contacts will be transitory, but others will establish themselves on a more lasting basis. Among the latter are the *Guides*. Each member of the circle will probably be shown to have at least one, and perhaps several, Guides. A Guide may be a spirit who has been associated with you for a long time whether you had any idea of this or not, maybe a relative such as a grandparent.

Each Guide has another function besides, as "bodyguard" to his or her particular protege, or even to the circle as a whole. The Guide is supposed to screen every spirit who seeks to speak through that person, or in the circle, to ensure nobody can suffer physical or psychic harm through the contact and also that the due order of the circle shall be preserved. If you should have any kind of unpleasant experience in the circle, you are entitled to protest to your Guide.

Now and then, also, there will be other Guides, spirits drawn to the circle or to one of its members by some affinity or shared concern. They may stay for a longer or shorter period. Occasionally, one you might have thought was with you for life will surprise you with the announcement that he or she has to depart for "another level", and you lose contact forthwith. But the astral world is known to be a region of continual change and movement, and experience of it, including this experience, accords with that knowledge.

The Guides will instruct and advise, not infrequently making suggestions about the procedure or the organization of the circle. The leader of the circle sometimes needs considerable tact in deciding what should be done, if anything, about these suggestions. Some may be excellent, some useless, but all tend to be given with an air of wise authority.

We have to keep our sense of proportion—and our sense of humor—about the Guides. A few really are "high and powerful," *but they are never all-knowing,* and usually they aren't much nearer to that condition than they were in their earthly lifetimes. Sometimes, too, even the wisest seem to have forgotten what it's like to be limited by material circumstances; but still their knowledge of their particular conditions goes beyond ours, they bring in the ideas and viewpoints of outside observers, and their friendship and enthusiasm deserve consideration. Many of them, we must add, show an engaging sense of humor themselves.

The Guides are not the only beings responsible for the organization of these spirits. There are also the *Controls*. These are concerned entirely with the spirits and not with the earthly circle, so they make an appearance more rarely; but occasionally they intervene to wield authority over Guides and other spirits alike.

So much organization among the spirits may surprise you, and from time to time you are likely to hear of even more extensive and powerful forms of organization among them. IS IT as great and stable as it seems?—or is it just another manifestion of the complex and changeful astral world? We may wonder; but certainly our spirit friends are very "human"! A spiritualist circle attracts its distinctive "spirit contacts," and in time you find that many aspects of its running, and its general atmosphere, are influenced by its "invisible organization." (That is a main reason why no two circles ever remain exactly alike for very long.)

"Inter-plane" Activites
More inspiring aspects of spirit communication are those which deal with teaching and healing. A number

of mediums have become notable as the intermediaries of spirits desiring to pass on the benefits of their understanding or their skill, and these benefits have been appreciated by many recipients.

Another outstanding aspect of spiritualism, and indeed one of its main activities, is concerned with helping some of the spirits themselves. Most often they want nothing except for a message to be given to a particular person, but sometimes there is a problem situation they want looked after.

It may be a simple thing, like wanting their photograph kept on someone's table, or a more difficult thing like wanting a house to be kept in their family. *All you generally can do is just to give the message to the people concerned.* If they in turn ask something, like, "Does he say how we're to afford the house?", you can, naturally, pass that question back to the spirit and it may be dealt with—*if you get the chance!*

Energy

Plenty of readily available astral energy is needed to bridge the gap between the incarnate and the discarnate, to enhance the prospect of communication. In the dynamic psychic ambience of the united group, there is naturally a free circulation of energy and/or astral substance; but if during a sitting a new build-up of energy is desired, the leader can direct a simple linking of hands for this purpose, for a period of two minutes or more, in order to strengthen the "emotional tide" of the circle.

(There is nothing new about the concept of energy being provided to enable spirits to communicate, although the methods used by modern spiritualists are somewhat restrained by comparison with other human endeavors. Many of the world's great "possession" cults, such as shamanism, Santeria, and the cult of Dionysus, use, and have used, strenuous dancing to aid this essential flow of energy. Again, Virgil tells how the hero Aeneas, going to consult the spirit of his father as to the future, made an offering of blood so the "shade" might gather strength and speak to him.

Different lands and ages show us different customs, but the general significance is the same: vital energy, of the kind which once linked the souls of the departed to their own physical bodies, is needed if they are to come into manifestation sufficiently for us to be aware of them. A person specially gifted as a "medium," that is as an intermediary between the planes of existence, usually has an abundance of free-flowing energy which will help in this way, but it is also true that an assembly of less energy-giving or less trained persons can, by combining their resources, jointly provide enough energy for good results.)

Aids and Signals
1. Incense

It is not always practicable to stop and link hands. Another and more continuous way of increasing the circulation of energy at sittings is to burn a suitable *incense.* This can be commenced as soon as members are arriving, so it can take effect throughout the sitting. Don't make the mistake of burning too great a quantity at one time; two moderate amounts are better.

Use joss-sticks or cones, in a suitable holder; these forms of incense are effective without a need for frequent attention. Sandalwood and patchouli are popular, and there are many other odors with which you can experiment. When you find an incense which suits your group, *keep to that particular kind as far as you can.* The accustomed fragrance will come to be a further "signal" announcing that your sitting is taking place, a nostalgic "call" both to sitters and to visitants.

Sensory signals are important because they appeal to the unconscious mind. The hypnotist has discovered this secret, and can confidently say to his subjects "When the light comes on you will do so-and-so," or "When the bell rings you will go to sleep." Granted, we are not using hypnotism, but we are going along very much with our unconscious mind and, with a little time and patience, it will respond to our signals just as to those of the hypnotist.

The spirits will respond similarly, because almost all of those we encounter will be entirely on the emotional and instinctual level, much as in a dream state.

With our incense, moreover, we are going further than the hypnotist's bell or lights. Certainly *any* sensory signal can be effective in calling a response from the unconscious mind, but neither visual nor auditory signals will make so direct a contact with it as will an odor. Children, and those adult human beings who live in primitive surroundings, make considerable use of their sense of smell, while their emotional and instinctual nature is also much nearer the surface than most of us have kept ours. So, for any of us, a signal through the sense of smell will more swiftly and powerfully pass the barriers of rationality than will a signal through any of the other senses.

2. The Power of Song

Another good traditional means of liberating energy in the spiritualist circle is *music*, and especially *song*. Taped, non-vocal music finds its best place at the beginning of the meeting: it welcomes, soothes, makes a harmonious background, and fills awkward gaps before the sitting. But from then on, song is best.

Hymns are fine if your group likes them, but even so, choose carefully! Some hymns are downright negative, and gentle piety may kill energy; but a hymn which combines high aspiration with vivid imagery and rhythmic melody will work wonders. Other songs than hymns may be chosen but the requirements are much the same. Make sure everyone present can feel comfortable with the sentiment, the tune and the pitch, and beyond that don't worry overmuch about the esthetic effect.

The choice of music will not be left entirely to

you or to your circle. There's likely to be a Guide, or other frequent visitant, who insists on some favorite song whenever he or she manifests, and this song may be anything from an anthem to rock. You can but accept it with good will; vigorous lung power sends the energy soaring, and whatever their musical tastes, energy is what the visitants most appreciate.

3. Light

Another traditional and effective aid, which is almost a distinctive feature of spiritualist procedure, is the use of *red light.* A lamp with a deep red bulb or, failing that, a red shade, is most helpful at the sitting, both for the stirring up of energy and to aid the astral sight. It should not, at the beginning of the meeting, be the only light in the room; people need to be able to see each other distinctly, to write in comfort any notes they may need about future meetings or such matters, and to be sure of their bearings in respect of the furniture. When the sitting itself is about to commence, however, the change of lighting can be a valuable signal of the change of mood. (But why not experiment with this? Your circle might like to see how they get on during a few sittings with a BLUE light—the *astral* color—instead of red.)

The Closing

A brief formality should close the sitting; everyone stands, the Guides and other spirit friends are thanked, and a blessing is pronounced upon all "until we meet again." Finally, the leader should clap hands loudly several times, to break the former frame of mind and to recall everyone to a fully normal state of consciousness. Simplicity, good sense and a touch of graciousness are the keynote, and usually nobody has anything but happy memories to carry away.

Possible Problems in the Circle

If the Guides are doing their work, nothing contrary need ever happen. Sometimes in an inexperienced group (with inexperienced guides!) an elemental, that is, a non-human nature spirit, gets into the circle, attracted by the free-flowing energy and the hospitable feeling of the group. "What's wrong with elementals?" —*Nothing whatever* in their natural surroundings, but they are likely to be disruptive in the circle. Their power to scan people's visualized images, and their able mimicry, can be deceptive; but they have little sense of human probability, and their craving for energetic activity which exceeds that of any human spirit, easily betrays them.

Don't take time however to make sure your noisy or violent guest really is an elemental; if *any* entity becomes too boisterous or causes disturbance and distress to members of your circle, request that entity, on a first occasion, to behave well or depart; if there is a second occasion, then you must order departure. In either case, too, address the Guides and ask their help

—they shouldn't have let it happen.

Sometimes, too, you are likely to encounter the problems of spirits who don't know where they are or what they're supposed to be doing. This is often the case where death has been sudden and not fully realized. You can meet with a sad person who wonders why none of his family will speak to him since he was hit by a car. He needs to understand they don't see or hear him; he can be advised to talk to them while they are asleep, for example. Or you may meet with the exuberant ones, very likely several together, who've just realized their disembodied state and their first reaction is to imagine all the pranks they can play.

These incidents are comparatively uncommon however, and most of the incidents which unfold themselves in the course of a sitting will be easier to cope with. The departed are, after all, not so very different from their incarnate counterparts.

Above all, those who take up spiritualist practices in conjunction with the program of psychic development given in this book, need have no fear of the worst types of experience which we sometimes hear of as besetting people in circle. The spiritual, mental and psychic health of one who regularly performs the Tabor Formulation and the Reflection on the Psychophysical Unity is too robust and well-balanced to attract or give ingress to harmful entities.

Looking Fairly at Spiritualism

Whether you've fully resolved to take your spiritualist development seriously, or whether you feel you'd like to know more about it, your best course is to go to two sittings—a public one and a private one—given by the best professional medium you can locate. This is not only for the sake of seeing how things are done and of getting the flavor of regularly-conducted spiritualist activity. Those things are important and you should take note of them, but even more important is the fact that some forms of psychism are "contagious"—they are to some extent transferable, or at least they can be intensified, by contact with a competent person. If at first you find you've also acquired, temporarily, a few of that medium's mannerisms, don't worry; you'll soon develop your own style, and the important thing is, as in swimming, to have made a start.

BUT IS MEDIUMSHIP WHAT IT SEEMS TO BE, WHAT THE SPIRITUALIST POSITION CLAIMS IT IS?

This isn't a question about "fraudulent mediums." Fraudulent mediums exist, and a very problematical set of people they are; for it's a known fact, also, that anyone who goes through the correct motions may on occasion give a "true message," just as any road-user who is headed the right way can in emergency be asked to carry an important few words. Generally, they seem stuck at a "get-up-and-talk" stage of development.

Our question is, What do genuine mediums really do?

We know that in communications or manifestations which take place in a spiritualist circle, much of the energy and astral substance come in any case from the medium and the other sitters. This has long been recognized. We know also that when a spirit speaks through a medium, not only the medium's physique and vocal chords will affect the result, but frequently his or her temperament and mode of speech, even habitual turns of phrase, may be involved also.

These latter peculiarities are admittedly hard for the skeptical to accept, but they need not result from either fraud or "split personality." The claim is, after all, that the spirit is taking over a *whole living person* as instrument, and in the lighter trance states is not even taking over completely. What happens is that the spirit makes contact with the medium at that level of the psyche which is most accessible to telepathy: the emotional and instinctual unconscious. From there, the communications flood into consciousness along the same "channels," and in the same way, as an idea of the medium's own; except that trance, like a dream state, clears a lot of obstructive rationalism out of the path.

There is some notable evidence in support of this explanation. Here is a brief example from a famous series of communications, in which the spirits identified themselves as deceased psychic investigators. One of the receiving mediums "received" a Greek word, *Thana-tos* ("death") which was entirely outside her knowledge.

Had she known that word subliminally—that is, had she heard it once and unconsciously stored it up, as children sometimes do with strange words—she'd probably have gotten the word itself right but used it in a wrong context; instead, the word was rightly used but her first spelling of it was *Sanatos* and then she corrected it. (She was doing automatic writing, a form of mediumship in which a pencil or pen is held and the hand is allowed to wander over a piece of paper without being guided or watched.) This word, previously unknown and at first incorrectly rendered, coming up in a thoroughly scholarly context, was part of a network of intricately inter-related messages, all calculated to show they were not the product of any incarnate participant's mind.

Now we are learning more about altered states of consciousness, the idea of different personalities within one individual—emanating from different components in the psyche—seems less strange than in the past. In some instances, without any doubt, material has been produced from a personality different from the medium's accustomed one, *but yet belonging to the medium.* And, given that we are all fundamentally capable of telepathy, telekinesis and prediction (to name only a few potentials), this hypothetical personality could produce some quite startling phenemena.

Yet, despite such possibilities in embodied human

nature, many people are convinced there is more in spirit communication than that. WHY?

In the last analysis, the verdict rests with the recipients of spirit communication. The touchstone is RECOGNITION. There is nothing conclusive in a medium's giving facts known only to Mr. X. and his deceased father; the medium could have them from Mr. X.'s mind by telepathy. There is nothing conclusive in the medium's warning Mr. X., in his father's name, of some danger: the medium is more likely to be prophetic than is Mr. X.'s father, who was never known as a seer in his lifetime. But if something in the style of the message strikes Mr. X., or if an entire personality comes through, and Mr. X. says with conviction *"That is my father,"* his statement is unassailable.

It is not that those who have passed on are totally unchanged. In a subtle sense, inevitably they have changed—*they are, truly, in an "altered state of consciousness."* But that only makes our sense of recognition the more definite and unmistakeable. It can happen rather similarly in earthly life: if our friends are as we've always known them, our recognition of them may never be a conscious act. But if Ed has grown a beard, and Sue comes along with a new hair-do, and their clothes are different—we consider and—*yes of course*—these ARE the people we've always known! The precise flavor, the mode of a personality, these are something we can never put into words, or prove, but we recognize them none the less surely.

We may perceive different facets of the personality at different times, but its identity is constant.

That is, and always has been, in every culture where mediumship has existed, its main strength and its greatest boon. Counsel, healing, foreknowledge, blessing, these are customarily found in the cult of the departed, but they are not its chief point. True, little may be given of high wisdom, and "survival" as demonstrated cannot prove immortality; but for many people one step at a time is enough. What is sought, and treasured when it is found, is this shining gem of recognition; the knowledge that the great transition has kept those we love so they can still recognize us, and we them.

SEANCE RECORD

Name of Group _____ Date _____

Name of Leader _____ Time start _____ end _____

Incense _____ Music _____ Lighting _____

Songs _____

Reminder of Sequence: 1. Tabor Formulation by all.
                                  2. Leader gives aspiration and then
                                         invokes Blessing & Protection.
                                  3. Music, Singing, Energy arousal, etc.
                                  4. Communications.
                                  5. Closing with Thanks and Blessing.

Guides _____

Medium(s) _____

Communications:

Phenomena:

Notes:

Checkpoint
6

- If you wish to employ spiritualist methods, for maximum effectiveness keep up your basic psychic development program.

- Plan your sitting to last at least one hour, even when you and your group are beginners in it.

- Follow the opening Tabor Formulation with a short invocation of divine blessing and protection.

- Light trance comes to members of the circle as a result of sitting quietly and letting the mind become stilled, together with the "atmosphere" of the circle, the group's psychic unity, and the known purpose of the sitting. (Light trance may not be recognized, by the subject or by others.)

- The leader of the circle should remain watchful and fully aware of the proceedings.

- During the sitting, those who feel impelled to speak should do so without reflection.

- Nobody should *try* to go into deep trance. Given a true contact, deep trance may in some circumstances supervene.

- The "Guides" are spirits who look after the circle or particular members; you will get to know them by degrees. They should be vigilant as to the spirits who gain admission, and they will help and advise to the best of their ability. But always remember they aren't all-knowing, and final responsibility remains with the incarnate leader.

- To raise extra energy in the circle at any time it is convenient, ask for a simple linking of hands for two minutes or more.

- Increase the available energy also by the use of
    Incense (joss sticks or cones)
    Suitable song
    Red light (experiment with blue, too.)

- Close the Circle simply and graciously, and ensure everyone returns to normal consciousness.

- Problems can sometimes arise in a circle, but you and your group have two strong protections: the aid you are entitled to expect from your Guides, and, above all, the power bestowed by your psychic development program.

- If you can arrange it, go to a private sitting and a public one given by the best professional medium you can find. The experience will do much to attune you to spiritualist procedure and attitudes.

Study Points

7

1. Dowsing, like other psychic abilities, is inborn in every person, and—like other psychic abilities—operates at the emotional-instinctual level.
   a. The dowsing ability is released into activity by an absorption of the attention, which inhibits the monitoring function of the rational mind.
   b. The equipment used in dowsing, as that used in most other psychic work, provides a necessary focal point for the attention and a means to magnify and show the orientation of inward movement.

2. The key to dowsing is at the astral levels of the psyche and the external universe.
   a. The forces which the dowser encounters, and which lead him to his goal, are of the astral world.

1. This is why the dowser may encounter "remanence"—the astral impressions of something no
longer existing on the material plane.
2. Likewise, the astral world also holds impressions of "the shape of things to come" which
can confuse the dowser.

b. In all cases, it is the astral "counterpart" that
is encountered by the dowser—that of presently
existing material objects, as also the astral phantasms of past objects and the foreshadowings of
future objects.

3. The movement of the dowsing instrument is produced
by a form of telekinesis that is directed by the unconscious mind of the operator.

a. The instrument must be held in some particular
manner.

b. It is preferable to make your own instrument,
choosing the materials carefully and shaping them
lovingly and with pride so that the imagination
can work along with the instrument as an expression of inward powers.

1. Various instruments, and their easy construc-
tion, are described fully in the text—as is
their proper usage.

4. To begin developing your dowsing ability, it is important to communicate your desire to your emotional-instinctual astral self, recognizing it as the

source of this psychic ability.

a. Your meditation exercises, your diet and lifestyle changes, your contacts with the worlds of nature, humanity, and your inner self should all be continued.

5. Actual dowsing involves:
   a. The "directive"—a small sample or token of what you are seeking.
   b. "Self-programming"—
      1. Holding the directive in your hand, focus your mind and emotions on the full reality of that which you are seeking—seeing it in your mind and feeling the good that will come from it.
      2. Then take up the dowsing instrument and "talk" to it—telling it how you value it and what it is you are seeking and why. Make it come "alive" for you: it is your partner, and it will guide you to your goal.
   c. Carry the directive in a convenient pocket while you are actually dowsing so that its subtle vibrations establish an affinity with the object you are searching for.
   d. "Listen" to the dowsing instrument as you work with it—it is the representative of your own astral being communicating with you by means of a sign language.
      1. You will need to discover the "code" of the movements which express its meaning.

e. Focusing your attention on your instrument, holding it in the particular way required, and "listening" to it—all work to induce a special altered state of consciousness during which the ordinary consciousness that is closely linked to the material world is lulled, and the astral being —with its link to the astral world—comes to the surface.

1. The astral level of the psyche can experience the astral level of whatever concerns it: that's why we use the directive.

6. Just as we used the directive to represent the object being sought, so can we substitute a map for the actual area to be dowsed, and with a pendulum as the instrument locate objects or persons sought.

a. In a similar fashion, a doll or picture can represent an actual person, and with the pendulum we can locate an injury or disease center in that person.

7. As with the other psychic abilities, practice is important, and the games described in the text are good starting points for developing the basic sensitivities that are part of dowsing.

7

A Search in
Two Worlds

There are some things, as there are some people, whose reputation has been boosted by their enemies far higher than their friends would ever dream of setting it. The motivation of these enemies is generally either vanity or fear, or both; that which they can neither explain nor defeat, that which they fear, must be of the greatest magnitude and mystery.

One form of activity which has been the object of this undesirable crying-up, is *dowsing*. Dowsing certainly is a most valuable ability and it often gives results whose accuracy and scope astonish the newcomer; but it is not "incredible" nor "supernatural" nor any of the other epithets which have been allotted to it by the skeptics. Dowsing is, as a fact, one of the most "natural" things a human being can do, belonging to the vital levels of our subrational existence.

Most usually a person seeking for water, minerals or anything else by this method will use either a rod or a pendulum as an indicator; but these things, like the hands of a clock, are useful only to magnify and to show the orientation of the inward movement.

There are a certain number of dowsers who, even without any such indicators, experience almost convulsive bodily movements when detecting whatever the object of their search may be. More experience tingling or burning sensations in different parts of the body; nor are any of these reactions triggered by the conscious awareness of the presence of the object, for many examples show unmistakeably that the reaction precedes its interpretation.

James A., for instance, a man personally known to the authors, had never thought of himself as a water-finder. Such a possibility would not greatly have interested him, and he had no reason to imagine it until some painful circumstances led to his talent being discovered for him.

To begin with, he had a violent fall and cracked a couple of his lower ribs. These were set and healed normally, and he returned to his ordinary occupations. Inevitably, as with any fractured bones, he suffered, and expected at first to suffer, a certain amount of discomfort; what troubled him more and more was the fact that as he moved around at home he experienced now and then most violent twinges of pain from the mended ribs, and this particular experience seemed not to lessen as time went by.

Back he went for re-examination, but no medical cause for his affliction showed up. In the end, when he explained that apart from an occasional twinge when traveling his sufferings were all produced by walking from front to back of his house or vice versa, he was referred for psychiatric examination.

Now it was his psyche which was inspected inside and out, although with no immediate result. The psychiatrist however was an up-to-date intelligent man who mentally cross-referenced every fact which came his way, and at last by this method he found himself a clue.

Among the mass of wildly various details he'd collected from James in the hope one of them might prove fertile, somewhere was a statement that James always had his worst moments of pain when passing a certain crack in the wall of his hallway. Once again the evidence was sifted for negative associations to cracks in walls, but there was nothing much. So the psychiatrist looked at it another way. James A's ribs hurting, and the crack in the wall, were related. *How?*

Why was the crack there? he asked James.

Because the house had settled in the middle.

Why had the house settled that way?

Directed to put in some research on this, James discovered the existence of an underground stream he'd never known about. So, his lower ribs shifted each time he crossed that hidden water; and, because they had been fractured, they hurt badly. And so, he was a born water-finder and hadn't known about that either.

In reality, like every other psychic talent, *the ability to dowse is inborn in every person* to some extent, even though—again like the other abilities—some individuals have it in an already more developed state than others do. Such experiences as that of James A., however, naturally lead people to inquire what this mysterious ability called dowsing really consists in, and which of its characteristics enable us to identify its nature and the means by which it can be cultivated.

A favorite hypothesis with those who wish to seem scientific without examining the evidence for themselves, and one which tends to be applied to a number of subjects including dowsing, is that of "unconscious muscular movement." The idea is that the unconscious mind of the operator determines (by whatever means) the answer to the question, or the direction of the object of the search, and transmits through the nerves a series of extremely subtle impulses to the muscles, as a result of which they produce the appropriate movements. Aside from the fact that James A. (for example) wasn't searching for anything and wasn't asking any questions, it is not at first easy to fault that hypothesis: however, we shall find that the true cause of the movements of the body and/or the instrument in dowsing is quite other.

The keys to dowsing are to be found in the astral level of the psyche and of the external universe:—

1. Dowsing is a faculty of the emotional-instinctual (astral) level of the psyche, released into activity by a complete absorption of attention which inhibits the monitoring function of the rational mind. This is certainly an altered state of consciousness, although not generally recognized as such.

What name is given to that state does not matter. Try, for instance, speaking to a person occupied in some creative skill, or to a mathematician or physicist pondering some abstract problem, or to a child building a castle with toy blocks, or to a pair of young lovers daydreaming about their future. *You probably can't get through to any of these people, and even if they answer you sensibly they may remember nothing of it later, like people who have been spoken to while aroused temporarily from sleep.* The dowsing state is very close to that, and the equipment helps in achieving that state by providing a necessary focal point for the attention.

2. Dowsing is dependent on the astral world for the impressions which lead the dowser to his or her goal. Although the dowser's quest is most often for something in the material world, the forces which are encountered, and which indicate the direction of that goal, *are not of the material world* (as the influence of the magnetic north upon a compass *is,* for instance) *but of the astral world.* This is demonstrated by some peculiarities in the mode of operation of those forces.

A good dowser has a high score of accurate findings, and so long as this accuracy is maintained we have no way of showing where the information comes from; but everyone slips up sometimes, and many of the mistakes made by dowsers are very instructive for that reason.

"Remanence"

One type of error comes up so often that dowsers have coined a word for its cause: *remanence.* In simple terms, this means "the tendency of conditions to remain." *Dowsers tend to pick up impressions of bygone objects as if those objects were still there;* a dowser seeking a building, for instance, might easily locate a site where such a building had stood long before. The dowsing instrument could react so as to give not only the plan of the foundations (which could still be physically present, if only as a disturbance in the ground) but also the height and particulars of the elevation.

Now, that building just isn't there to be measured —*in the material world.* All its "remaining," which can give through dowsing the same reactions as a solidly existing building, *is in the astral world.*

Besides the shapes of things past, the astral world holds also "the shape of things to come," and on occasion these images too can confuse the scene for the dowser; at first they are no more recognizable for what they are, than the vestiges of the past.

Why is the dowser not able to distinguish those

astral phantasms from the material objects which he is searching out? Because in the astral world, along with those lingering traces of the past and foreshadowings of the future, *there is also the astral counterpart of everything* presently *existing in the material world*; and it is THAT COUNTERPART, not the material world itself, which the dowser's emotional-instinctual nature is aware of. This area of the psyche, being our astral level within, *perceives its kindred world just as our physical senses perceive theirs.* By some psychic techniques, the astral perception is brought through into consciousness; in dowsing, it is instead signalled in movements. *But these signals are apt, on occasion, to be triggered by the astral images of the past or future, exactly as they normally are by the astral counterparts of* present *material objects.*

3.   Dowsing is dependent on the astral level of the psyche for the movement imparted to the instrument: not through the muscles, but directly.

THIS MOVEMENT IS PRODUCED BY A FORM OF TELEKINESIS: TELEKINESIS DIRECTED BY THE UNCONSCIOUS MIND OF THE OPERATOR AND NOT, AS IN THE CASE OF ORDINARY TELEKINESIS, BY THE CONSCIOUS MIND.

The hypothesis of "unconscious muscular movement," previously mentioned, doesn't stand up to the facts; here are some it completely ignores:

People who use a dowsing instrument of the form of a loop or fork (these will be described in the next section of this chapter) have been known to have their fingers and palms blistered and even lacerated in some circumstances when the instrument moves violently and they are trying to keep it under control. At that time the instrument is clearly moving *against* their muscles, not *with* them. Nor is it an example of hand working against hand, for when the fork or loop twists around it moves *in the same direction against each hand*; besides, when the dowser uses "angle-rods" each hand holds a separate rod so no interaction of the hands would then be possible, yet the violence of the movement is sometimes just as great.

So as to guard against hand injury, which could be particularly unpleasant with metal rods, people who use that type of equipment frequently fit them with "sleeves," in which the rods turn almost freely. No movement of the rods except for a weak swing to this side or that could in those circumstances be produced by a less-than-conspicuous movement of the hands, whether conscious or otherwise.

Furthermore, as pointed out in Chapter 3, tele-kinetic force is characterized by the fact that distance makes an appreciable difference to its action. This too is a conspicuous feature of dowsing.

Equipment

Some seekers for water or for metals use no equipment at all. The influences which guide them to what they seek are felt in their physical body, either as a movement of the bones—as James A, discovered—or as a sensation of heat in the numberless tiny nerve-endings in soles or palms.

These people have never had, or have managed to shed, the tendency of the rational consciousness to prevent the emotional-instinctual nature from physically signalling its findings. They are able to act almost as spontaneously as does a thirsty animal (or even a plant) moving towards the life-sustaining fluid. For most civilized folk, however, the instrumentality of dowsing equipment is an important factor in success. It gives to the consciousness a necessary focal point.

No matter what kind of equipment you use in dowsing, you have to hold it in a particular way, in a stressed or at least careful manner; and you have to keep your attention upon it, moment by moment, for the way it may be moving or for what it may indicate.

Types of Dowsing Equipment

The importance of your dowsing equipment doesn't mean it has to be costly or elaborate. There is an old saying, that a bad workman blames his tools; it is also true that the good workman won't start in on a job without tools he can take a pride in—even if it's a pride in being able to use such primitive gear skill-fully and effectively! So make your own dowsing equipment; choose your materials carefully and shape them lovingly, and above all have *something that your imagination can work along with*, a means of expression to your inward powers.

Possible forms of dowsing equipment, other than the pendulum, include angle-rods, a loop of stout rattan or flexible cane, the traditional fork of wood, and V- or Y-shaped pieces made from synthetic materials (of which nylon, being both flexible and tough, is still probably best). Remember James A.'s experience with his own ribs!—something of that nature, thin, pliant, partly free and partly fixed, is what you are seeking.*

1.   ANGLE-RODS are easy to make. You need two pieces of wire (mild steel or other suitable metal), thick enough to keep its form and flexible enough to be bent without cracking; each piece some fifteen inches long. Bend each wire to a right angle at about one third the distance along its length, so one leg of the angle is five inches long and the other ten inches. The exact dimensions don't matter, but it does matter that the two finished rods should be as nearly identical as you can make them. *Make sure the two five-inch legs are entirely smooth and free from snags, sharp points or edges, because this is the part which will*

---

*There exist many books on dowsing, from most of which something useful or stimulating can be gained. The following titles are singled out, not to exclude other good books on the subject, but because these give details of a variety of instruments and techniques: *Techniques of Swing-rod Dowsing* by Bill Cox (published by "Forces", Santa Monica, CA) 1977; *Dowsing for Everyone* by Harvey Howells (Stephen Green Press, Brettleboro, Vermont) 1979; *Modern Dowsing* by Raymond C. Willey (Esoteric Publications, Sedona, Arizona) 1975.

be twisting around in your grip when you use the rods.
If you wish, you can fit them with "sleeves," which will
to a great extent obviate this problem; but even so,
you still need to ensure the rods will rotate smoothly
in the sleeves.

These sleeves are simply tubes of cardboard or
plastic, just slightly shorter than the five-inch legs over
which they have to fit, and wide enough to allow free
movement to the rods while being convenient to grip.
The end of the leg should be flattened, turned over, or
enlarged by some other means to keep the sleeve from
becoming detached.

2.   The CANE OR RATTAN LOOP is made from a piece
of tough, whippy vegetable stem about twenty-seven
inches long; it needs to be bound securely with thin
cord or strong synthetic string, in two stages as shown
below. The loop and the two ends alike will need to
be held steady by human or mechanical agency, while
the loop is bound securely as shown in Figure 1 and
tied off, then bound as illustrated in Figure 2 and
securely tied off once more.

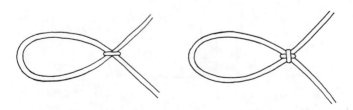

Fig. 1   Fig. 2

Jeanne Lord Westbrook

3. The traditional DOWSING FORK presents an initial difficulty, that of finding a suitable small branch to cut. Hazel, willow and the fruit-woods are all good for keeping their resilience, not drying out and becoming brittle too soon after cutting; but hazel and willow also are conspicuous for growing twigs with a sufficiency of straight length between outgrowths, which is not always the case with the fruitwoods. You need your fork to have at least ten inches of straight, clear wood about one-half inch in diameter, dividing into a symmetrical fork which you can trim into two equal prongs about five to eight inches long.

In preparing your branch as a dowsing fork, make the short ends as smooth and clean as you can, since in use they are likely to twist around in your hands. But don't strip off the bark, or the wood will quickly become dry, rigid and unresponsive. When you have trimmed the fork to your requirements, melt some candle ends in a can, and, while keeping the wax at a high enough temperature, dip each in turn of the three cut ends of the fork into the melted wax. Leave it there long enough for the adjacent wood to soak up the wax, then remove. When the absorbed wax sets, it will seal the end and so help the fork retain its moisture and flexibility. If you can't for any reason use the melted wax, use corn oil, olive or (best of all) linseed oil, warmed, to soak and seal the ends of the fork.

4. The next type of dowsing instrument which must

be mentioned is the FORK OF MAN-MADE MATERIALS. (Wooden lath can be included here, too.) Any straight lengths of tough, light-weight, flexible material are worth trying, and some are excellent. Two plastic pointers, for instance, will serve the purpose well.

With many types of rod or strip, there is no need to form a V- or Y-shape; you may have to cut convenient lengths—about twenty inches, less or more according to general bulk and proportion—but no further shaping is required. Place them side by side, and, starting at one end, cement and/or bind them together through about two-thirds or three-quarters of their length, as you may choose. Even if the pieces are glued together securely, it is still a good idea to put a few turns of strong thread or wire to bind them at what will be the point of greatest stress: that is, at the juncture of the glued section with the free ends. Then, to use the instrument, you simply take the free ends one in each hand, as will be described below, and pull them apart.

5.   The remaining rod-type instrument for dowsing to be included here is, somewhat surprisingly, a minority choice: the SINGLE WAND. This can be of any material—wood, metal, synthetic—if it be long, straight, slender, flexible and of moderate weight. A lecturer's pointer, an antenna for television or radio, a slender bamboo, or, again, a curtain rod but this time of round cross-section, all make acceptable

"wands." Don't pass up a chance to make or adapt for yourself a dowsing instrument of this probably most ancient form; you may be one of those people for whom it becomes the favorite!

All the dowsing instruments described above work best in the conditions for which they were developed: that is, you should be walking about in the open air. Practice in other conditions can be disappointing and therefore discouraging, but there is no reason why you shouldn't "go through the motions" indoors if you wish, for practice in holding the instrument.

Go outdoors however, and preferably into the open country, to practice properly as soon as you can. If you can go in the company of an experienced dowser, so much the better!

The method of using the *angle-rods* is illustrated on page 180. In holding them, the thumb rests upon the top joints of the forefinger, and beside the top of the sleeve; the fingers grip only the sleeve, so that the angle-rod will rotate within this almost free from friction.

The loop, and the various types of fork, are all held in one way: with one of the fork ends in each hand, and the loop or rod pointing upwards. This should involve a certain amount of tension in the instrument (whether the instrument be natural or man-made) as the free ends are pulled away from the central axis. One of the traditional methods is illustrated on page 184,

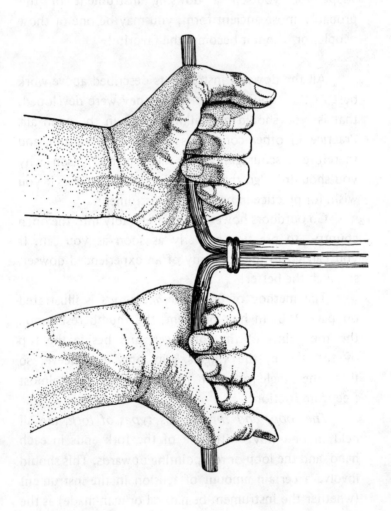

but you should experiment with it and discover what is best *for you.*

The simple wand has its own peculiarities. You hold it forward horizontally in one hand; usually your stronger hand but some people get better results with the other. The interesting thing is that if your wand tapers to one end, *you should hold it by the more slender end, not by the thicker one.* That gives it more stress and "whippiness."

Beginning Dowsing
(1) Help from the Unconscious

When you want to begin developing the faculty of dowsing, your first concern should be to convey effectively to your emotional-instinctual nature that this skill is *necessary.*

An excellent way to do this is to take a time when you feel quiet and meditative; sit down then and *talk* —talk aloud, in all seriousness—to your astral being. Give it a warm greeting, tell it how gladly you recognize its presence, how much you cherish it and value its assistance at all times; then go over the reasons why learning to dowse is necessary to your happiness and life-style. Give an assurance, too, that this new ability is one in which your astral being will take a vital part, and will gain the means to communicate much of its hitherto mute knowledge and perceptions. Align yourself with all that you say as positively as you can, dwelling especially upon every emotional aspect of it. Speak gently, kindly, but with authority; be confident, so as to avoid both anxiety and casualness, and express yourself in simple words because your astral being is in some respects very childlike.

This address should be repeated from time to time, as you feel moved. As you begin to have success in developing the faculty and you acknowledge in this way the part played by your astral being, your recognition will encourage its further and more effective co-operation.

It's important, if you want to dowse competently, to keep up your regular meditations, keep up your good diet and simple life-style, keep up your contacts with the world of nature, the human world and the world within. These are important factors in all psychic development, but they have a special relevance to the powers we are discussing in this chapter.

(2) Before Setting Out

When you've made your first piece of dowsing equipment, be it loop, fork, wand or pair of angle-rods, all you can do with it in or around the house is just to get the feel of handling it, how this particular kind of instrument is to be gripped and carried when in use. For real practice in dowsing, however, you should go out into the right place, into the open country. (If that is impossible for you, at least at present, you have other options: later in this chapter there is a section on pendulum dowsing, which can open most exciting dimensions without crossing your threshold, and then some games to help you develop, and have different kinds of fun with, some of the same faculties that are used in dowsing.)

Before you set out on a dowsing expedition, there are some preparations to make. Whether you are a beginner or experienced, you will need a *directive*, and you will need *to program yourself*.

A. The Directive

A *directive* is a small sample, or token, of what you are going to search for: a little bottle of water for instance, a chip of whatever mineral, a sample coin or artifact, a few leaves if you seek a particular plant, or, no matter what may be your quest, its name in bold lettering on a piece of card. These are only a few example of possible directives; there is no end to their variety, and dowsers exercise great ingenuity sometimes in devising tokens to represent successfully something of which no sample can be had.

B. Programming Yourself

As shortly as possible before setting out on a dowsing expedition, you should spend some time alone with the directive and your dowsing instrument.

Hold the directive in your hand while you focus your mind, and especially your emotions, upon the full reality of that which you will be seeking, and upon the need for finding it. Let your imagination dwell upon various aspects of the object of your search, so as to make it as vividly present to you as possible. Conjure up in your imagination not only all the good qualities of the object of your search in itself, but also all the good that you can expect from its finding. Remember, your astral being, for which you are creating this image, is not attracted to abstract ideas but to simple, direct pictures and sense-impressions, and the simplest and most direct of emotions.

When you feel you have given sufficient time to this, lay down the directive and gently let the image or impressions you have built up fade from your consciousness; then take up your dowsing instrument.

Hold this, sometimes as you would while dowsing, sometimes in a tender, caressing manner, while you talk softly to it. Tell it how much you prize it, tell it of what you are going to seek and of the great importance, the necessity of finding it. Regard your dowsing instrument as a living entity with which you have an understanding, an affinity. You and it are partners; while you carry it, it will guide you. Speak to it of these matters, and while you do so, begin to walk about with it until you feel the bond between it and yourself is fully activated, the instrument is "awake."

(3) On Setting Out

If you can go, at least for your first few ventures in dowsing, with a friend who has a working ability in it, that will be the greatest help you could have.

With dowsing as with some other psychic powers, the more experienced and skilled in it is the person you set out with, the better you are likely to fare. At the same time, never forget the whole potential of dowsing is within YOU, and whatever the circumstances you can, with perseverance, cultivate it.

Besides your *dowsing instrument* and your *directive*, you should in any case have with you the following:

> *a map of the area*
> *a few useful tools* (as appropriate)
> *pen and notebook*

so you can locate at least roughly any interesting spot on your route, make notes, and enable yourself to keep a record, besides being able to collect, dig, measure or photograph as may be suited to your quest.

Carry your directive in a convenient pocket. During the time you are actually dowsing, you'll be intent upon watching your instrument. But your directive will be there with you all the time, maintaining its subtle vibrations of affinity with what you are looking for and conditioning your activity accordingly. *You don't have to keep consciously remembering that your directive is there; your astral being knows it is.* Whenever you take a rest from dowsing, however, you should use the opportunity to take out your directive, look at it and handle it.

Having arrived at your starting-point, don't set off in a rush. Take time to look over the landscape and to review mentally what you are going to do. If you feel any traces of tension, close your eyes and draw a few deep breaths, right in and right out, slowly; then you should be ready to begin. Take the dowsing grip on the instrument, and begin walking.

(When you are experienced, you may get an initial indication from the instrument about the direction. At first, the starting choice of direction is likely to be yours, or an experienced dowser's if there is one present.)

(4) The First Signals

As you walk along, you may not at first find it easy to settle into the serenity of mind which is right for dowsing. To a great extent, any unsettled feeling is likely to be due to an initial self-consciousness which will soon disappear; but another cause is likely to be that you don't quite know what your dowsing instrument is going to do, or when. Trust it, talk to it, attune yourself to it and it to you. *You will know the first dowsing signal when it comes!*

Until it comes, you'll not be sure whether any slight movement of the instrument might be a signal, or whether it might be caused by uneven ground, a gust of wind, a nerve jumping in your arm, or pure imagination. But when a real response occurs, it will be unmistakeable.

It will feel as though an invisible person had taken hold of the instrument and was trying to point it in a new direction, even to twist it out of your hands; or it may just give one sudden jerk. The distinctive thing is the feeling of "another person" causing the movement deliberately. At the same time, or just before the pull, you may get an "electric" tingling, or hot or creeping sensations somewhere in your body: arms, spine and feet are the likeliest areas.

Your next question will be, *What does this signal mean?*

If you are using angle rods, for instance, the long arms may twist outwards simultaneously. If you have a loop or a fork, it may insist on turning down or to one side. Or the free end of a wand may circle at frantic speed.

Does it say "You're on the right track" or "Stop here"? Is it "Turn"—perhaps "Turn around"—or "Dig"? The first time you receive a particular signal, your best plan is to go back a little way, then come up to the spot again, more slowly. This may result in your receiving the same signal, or a different one.

If no light is shed on the meaning by the new occurrence, you can again approach the spot but from a different angle, or you can ask the instrument whether the same meaning can be expressed by a different signal, or you can try doing what the signal LOOKS to you as though it means.

In such a situation, realize that the dowsing instrument has become the representative of *your own astral being*; and the intention of your astral being is NOT to set puzzles for you (however it may seem) but to use the dowsing instrument as a means to establish a

code for SPEAKING TO YOU BY SIGN LANGUAGE.
You need, therefore, to find out in quiet reflection
what is the most simple and natural meaning, *to your
astral being,* of this particular movement of the instrument. This is best done at the time, if possible;
your early experiments in dowsing will gain more value
from settling a few points of this kind, than from
mere mileage.

One complication is, however, possible. If your
early expeditions are made in the company of an experienced dowser, it's likely that this friend will be able
to tell you the meaning of every signal you receive
from the instrument. A complete "code" may
be given you in this way—the same one which exists
between your friend and his or her dowsing instrument.
Afterwards, when you go out dowsing alone, you will
be likely to find that the "code" changes in some particulars. Soon it will become *your own code,* the one
which is to be permanently established between *your*
dowsing instrument and *you.*

(5) The Interpersonal Aspect

Here is another well-known fact. Many people
who, from one cause or another, had real difficulty in
finding and developing their dowsing ability, have experienced a complete change in the situation when
they were helped by an established dowser, who placed
his or her hands upon their arms while they held the
fork. On approaching the sought-for objective they

felt the fork turn in their palms, sometimes violently.

Usually this procedure was repeated two or three times, then the learners were able to continue unaided.

That fact, and the one mentioned above, of the astral being of the learner temporarily adopting the "code" of the established dowser, are not very surprising when you realize how inter-related human beings are at astral level, especially when they share an avocation or other great interest. With regard to dowsing, fortunately there' is everything to gain from this, because dowsing is one of the most readily "contagious" of psychic powers: if an able dowser is helping you, you should rapidly get beyond the dependent stage and be able to discover your own direction. *And "your own direction" applies to more than the code with your dowsing instrument.*

Most dowsers, whatever their general standard of achievement, have one particular subject of search for which they are more successful than for any other. It may be missing persons, or oil, or fossils, or herbs —almost anything the world harbors! Nobody but you can discover your particular flair, and it may take time. Initially, you will probably go along with your friend's speciality, or the needs of your district, or the fashion of the day (for there are fashions in dowsing as in other matters.) However, when you *find yourself* there will be no doubt about your particular "idiom" of dowsing, your personal matter and manner of search.

In general, dowsing is not a conspicuously sociable activity. While dowsing, each person is necessarily limited to communication with the dowsing instrument, the representative of his/her astral being. If your group takes up dowsing, and if when members reach a degree of proficiency an expedition is organized to some specially interesting area of country (to dowse for archeological remains for instance, or for fossils or minerals, or to trace an underground watercourse or ore-vein, or to find useful plants) social fun must be limited to the period of rest and refreshment when dowsing is over. The expedition will, however, have the high exhilaration of a shared outdoor activity which brings mutually enhanced psychic power to all the participants.

(6) Exploration by Pendulum
A. A Valuable Psychic Technique

The pendulum can be used outdoors, suspended from the fingers, for the same purposes as a large-scale dowsing instrument. It is not recommended to be used in this way, only because in a wide landscape it may be less precise as a direction-finder than are the larger and more rigid instruments, and because a breeze might interfere with its working. Despite these disadvantages, it has been used in the open air with notable success, both alone and as an auxiliary to other instruments. It is in indoor work, however, that the pendulum really comes into its own; and this distinctive form of dowsing, besides being a valuable psychic technique in its own right, also throws more light on the nature of dowsing generally.

Whether indoors or out, if we use the pendulum as a dowsing instrument a great deal of the earlier part of this chapter will apply to it. We need means to associate ourselves with the intended matter of exploration, and the "directive" (or "Witness") method is highly effective. Whether dowsing by pendulum or other means, to have with us something representative of what is sought, and to advert to it from time to time as convenient, is a truly powerful means of getting our astral being, via the dowsing instrument, to lead us to our goal.

The level at which such directives "work" indicates that although in some respects we are here operating very close to the material level, *the faculty which is being employed is in fact a psychic one and not a physical one however subtle.*

For instance: supposing we are seeking a missing person. We can use as directive a garment or other article belonging to that person. A bloodhound setting out to track someone would likewise be given a garment or other article to sniff at. So, are we in our fashion using some ultra-refined and attenuated form of the sense of smell, or some related physical sense, in our dowsing?

NO! Instead of a garment, we can be given a photograph of the missing person, and this may be a print straight from processing, which that person has never touched or even seen. But the likeness is, emotionally and psychically, as potent a directive to guide us in our dowsing as any garment could be.

Much the same principles apply to a stretch of country, or to a building, about which you mean to do some dowsing. A visit is not always possible; in such cases the pendulum dowser can operate by means of photographs and a map.

Pendulum dowsing in particular thus has some major characteristics which can only be understood in terms of the essential interaction with the astral world in dowsing. If it is usual – as we consistently see it to be – for a dowser to go into a mildly altered state of consciousness through keeping the attention for long periods on the instrument, even more strongly and positively is such a state likely to be induced by focusing attention upon the silent rhythm of a pendulum. The ordinary consciousness, with its powerful link with the material world, is effectively lulled, so that the quiet and less aggressive activity of our astral being has more freedom to surface and to bring into effect its own natural link with the astral world.

And, because of the particular nature of the astral world, *a link with it is a link with the whole of it*, so that even without "astral projection" strictly so called, the astral level of the psyche can experience the astral level of whatever concerns it. *Theoretically at any rate there is no limit to this possibility.*

This last is a principle we see operating over and over in pendulum dowsing. People boggle and stumble over *how* pendulum dowsing gets at unknown facts, to such an extent that they very often find it more comfortable to deny the very occurrence of it; but the real trouble is that they are trying to see *how* in terms of the material world, when it is an astral-world function operating at its own level of cause and effect.

Thus, if you say a paper doll temporarily represents a given person's anatomy, and you get your astral being to accept this, then your pendulum, when you hold it over the paper doll, should indicate where that person hurts; and it will, if you have a flair for diagnosis. Or if you are seeking buried treasure and you have a map of a likely island, then your pendulum will indicate (again, if you have a flair for treasure-finding) as clearly on the map where the treasure is, as your dowsing fork would indicate it if you were physically to visit the island.

THESE THINGS HAPPEN. Numberless dowsers could tell their true histories of incidents along these lines. Their astral being is able by means of a symbol—the directive—to reach out to the reality, to contact it. Sometimes the dowser has a sense of making this contact, and sometimes there is no perception of it; but, either way, the pendulum registers the direction and locality found by the astral being.

The only limitation upon possibilities of this

kind is our astral being's conception of what concerns it. That is why, if we want our range of inquiry to extend beyond our immediate and spontaneous interests, a strong degree of communication with our astral being is essential.

B. The Initial Data

If you are planning some work at a distance, by pendulum, you should obtain maps, photographs, diagrams, as well as verbal descriptions. Ask questions to fill any gaps you can think of, particularly gaps in your visual impressions. *Don't worry about things you* can't *find out:* this is not an attempt on the part of your rational mind to do your astral being's work for it. You simply want to begin your explorations with the clearest possible data for your imagination.

Č. Seeking a Missing Person

If it is a person you seek, therefore, you want a vivid mental image of that person; not only a photograph, but also a clear idea of the personality, voice, interests, everything to make that person "present" to you. You need to associate those qualities strongly with the photograph or other directive.

You also need a large scale map of the area from which the person disappeared. You may also need a map of some other area if there's a strong presumption the person may have gone there, but otherwise you will do best in most cases to stay with the one map unless and until you get an indication on the direction of further search. Spread the first map out flat on a large table, and have your directive and any other photographs or possessions of the person to hand, preferably on a smaller table.

Before you begin dowsing, program yourself. Look at the map and note its main features; use your imagination to see it as an actual expanse of country as viewed from an airplane or helicopter. (You will use that concept again while dowsing, so accustom yourself to it now as much as you can.)

Take up your directive, gently turn your attention away from the map and give it to building up your sense of the person. Dwell on the reality of the person; imagine you see him or her in front of you. This person smiles, moves, speaks; you hear the sound of the voice. *Don't begrudge time to building up this image of the person;* you will not be able to do it to the same extent while you are dowsing, and you need to keep the "feel" of that person associated as strongly as possible with the directive.

When you have spent sufficient time with the directive, put it aside and take up your pendulum. Caress it, warm it in your hands, speak to it with a few words of friendly greeting, and then suspend it from your fingers. (It is best to place your directive close to the hand you'll *not* be using for the pendulum.) Talk to the pendulum about the missing person and why it is necessary to find this person. Remember to give the emotional reasons rather than the rational reasons, and at some point lay your free hand on the directive while you are softly talking to the pendulum.

Then, gently and without haste, carry the pendulum across the map so that it hangs right above the place the person disappeared from. (If there is any doubt about the details, choose the person's home as your starting point.)

Suspended thus, your pendulum will, perhaps at once, perhaps after a pause, take up a directional swing. *(You don't, of course, visualize the pendulum swinging.)* As there are two ends—turning-points— to the swing, you may have to check which direction is meant by this. If you don't have a technique for testing this point, try the following.

Smoothly and evenly, carry the pendulum to a point over one end of its former swing, and wait. If that is the correct direction to move in, the pendulum should continue swinging. If however you have taken it in the direction opposite to that of the person's travel, it should stop dead. Carry it back to the starting-point, wait until it takes up its former swing, then, slowly and gently, take it along the way it has indicated, until it changes direction.

Verify the exact point on the map where the change of direction takes place (this may be indicated by the pendulum circling when you hold it above the right spot), wait for resumption of the normal swing and then gently take it along in its new direction.

Sometimes the pendulum can react quite violently; it may circle violently over a place where the person stayed or now is, or it can swing violently in a particular direction, trying to get off the limits of this particular map altogether. The implications will be clear to you.

If at any time the movement falters or stops in an indeterminate manner, keep it suspended where it is while you renew your contact with the directive and renew your mental image of the person. At any stage of the procedure, talk softly to the pendulum about the search, about the places passed over—this will help keep the landscape real to you—and about the person sought for. The more completely you can imagine yourself out of the material world of map, chair and table, the more rapidly and decisively your pendulum is likely to tell its story.

Dowsing—a Conclusion

That example should give at least an idea of the scope and possibilities of pendulum dowsing. Not only every dowser, but every individual venture in dowsing, will produce distinctive variations in the requirements and in ways of meeting them. Once you have your basic "code" established, dowsing is as much an art of continual improvisation as is any dialogue. In any sphere of human inquiry, the possibilities are limitless; but the principles involved remain the same, and are very clearly intelligible, once the essential relationships *of the dowsing instrument with the astral being, and of the astral being with the astral world,* are accepted.

Pull, Glow and Swing
Astral Power Games for the Group

On first reading through this chapter, you may very likely decide you want to begin experimenting with instruments and getting into dowsing at once. Or the time of year may be wrong for a beginning of field-work, or there may be some other reason why you can't, or don't want to, make a start just now.

In that case, if you have a group, the games which follow offer at least a means of meeting with, and getting into practice with, some of the powers which are used in dowsing. If however you do begin to practice dowsing at once (which, if the conditions are at all right, is a good idea while the impulse is fresh and clear to you) these games again can be very interesting and helpful.

Thus you can use them in your group as an introduction, to get the feeling of these powers and forces before you take up dowsing; or you can use them to provide some variety in approach, and to keep up the united group spirit, when people are already into dowsing. They are, besides, good social fun for any time; the first two in particular being fine to "warm up" group energy for various occasions.

The first game, "Magnets", is an old High School favorite (unofficial!) although most people who have played it will probably not have thought much about what can be learned from it. *Try it, and find out how it feels to be a dowsing rod!*

Magnets
(best for 4, 5 or 6 players)

All the players except one form a circle; the remaining player—the "pin"—stands in the center, blindfolded or with hands over eyes.

The players in the circle silently agree to one of their number as the "magnet". Then each of them, the "magnet" included, lays the tip of a finger *lightly* upon the "pin". (No prodding, please!) The fingers may touch bare or clothed skin, it makes no difference.

Now each person in the circle thinks about the "magnet", or about the "pin" moving towards the "magnet"; the "magnet" will find the latter idea easier. The "pin" doesn't have to think, *and will do best not to speculate as to the direction of the "magnet"*.

A few minutes may pass while the circle "warms up". Then the "pin" will begin to sway out of vertical, to tilt in one direction or another; then will lean over further, will try to regain a balance, and at last will go conclusively over to the "magnet", who may have to lend a supporting arm!

Let two or three people in the circle try being "magnets", then let someone else have a turn at being "pin". This may bring out some new aspects of inter-relationships within the group:

Do all do equally well as "magnets"?

Or as "pins"?

Do some pairs do exceptionally well when one is "magnet" and the other "pin"?

And when they are the other way about?

Do people's results tally with their degree of friendship with each other?

You may have one or two instances of reverse effect: people who, when they are "pins", don't simply get it wrong but *almost always move in just the opposite direction from the "magnet".*

This peculiarity has much the same significance as getting a "lower than hazard" average with the ESP cards. There is distinctly a good degree of psychism in evidence, but it is being psychologically negated; either the situation, or some personal aspect of it, is uncongenial, or else this person at some level doesn't *want* to be psychic—but is developing all the same! You may never know the underlying facts, but all such things contribute to the human reality of your group.

After the initial game of "Magnets", have the players talk over their experiences, especially their experiences as "pins". (They will describe in their own ways how they were not pushed but, in fact, "magnetized"; it was not the pressure of the fingers which directed them, but some force which seemed to be working upon and through their whole body.)

In general, we can say that what happens to the "pin" is the same sort of action which occurs with a dowsing-rod!

By way of further experiment and added interest, you might try this variation too.

This game is organized just as in the original

version, except that the "pin" is NOT TOUCHED by the other players; each extends a finger towards him or her, but the fingertips remain about two inches away.

This requires some watchful moving with the "pin", so as to remain near but not to make contact. Many players find the effect exactly the same as with contact, the "pin" moving unerringly towards the "magnet", *but some "pins" have said they felt more conscious of the tension of force when the game is played this way.*

The purpose in the next game is to test whether persons who don't know which of many objects has been touched, can identify the right one by touching it themselves. This is very good experience for the aspiring dowser as well as for the budding psychometrist, giving an opportunity to *know,* rather than just to *believe in,* the reality of non-material influences.

Hot Trail
(Any number of players)

You know the way children ask "Hot or cold?" in a treasure hunt. You have to tell them they're "hot", or "getting warmer," when they are in the region of the treasure, "cold" when they move away from it.

In this game, nobody tells anyone if they are "hot or cold"; the player who is doing the hunting has to find out by ESP.

Draw lots, or by some agreed method decide who's to go out of the room. In that player's absence the remaining players decide, silently, on an object in the room. *Each person in the room then touches that object for a moment,* not thinking anything in particular; and all return to their places. The object has been "charged".

The player outside is re-admitted, and is at liberty to move around the room, touching various objects at will until the right one is discovered. Nobody is allowed to give any clues; the object has to be identified by the one player unaided.

Occasionally the game "shorts"; the player from outside will come right in and state, "The object is that picture," or "that pen," or whatever it is, thus scoring an easy point. Generally, however, after some experimenting, the player will find the sensitivity of fingertips which gives an awareness of the chosen and handled thing, and so will locate and name it.

Some people, on touching the right object, experience a sensation of heat; sometimes with this, or instead of it, there can be a magnetic pull. Having discovered the object, *the "hunting" player scores a point,* and remains as one of the company in the room while someone else takes a turn outside.

It's possible the "hunter" may guess wrong and may say "It's this!" when it is not. Wrong guesses are dealt with according to the number of players and the time available for the game; several mistakes, perhaps two or four, being allowed before the player is "out" on the next one. A player who is "out", having either guessed wrong at the final attempt or having exhausted his/her allotted time, rejoins the company without scoring.

The winner is the player with most points when everyone has had the same number of turns. If two or more players have the same score, judgment should be made in favor of the one out of those players who made the least number of wrong guesses.

Details of organization for this game are quite elastic, and can be decided in any group to suit its own needs; the above outline is a general guide.

This is a good game to come back to from time to time. Your group might introduce it at a party, too, after a little practice!

Now we have two pendulum games. There's a likeness between them, certainly, but there's also an important difference.

Whose?
A pendulum game
(any number of players)

Fit a fabric cover to a box or basket, so each person in turn can slip a hand under the cover to deposit two or three small objects which have been kept concealed.

Such objects can be quite trivial items: a small pencil, a pack of gum, a ring, a pocket-knife, matches, a pebble, even a small coin if the owner is quite sure of recognizing it again. (Someone else might put in one of the same kind!) Members of the group can have been asked beforehand to bring such items with them, and not to show them or name them to any other person present. Watches are generally found unsatisfactory, both for this and for psychometry practice; it may be because they have such an intense "life" of their own.

These items having been collected under cover, the players draw lots for their turns as pendulum operator. The first pendulum operator extracts an object at random from the box (if it happens to be one of the operator's own, it can be put back without comment and another one taken) and places it on the upturned palm of the nearest other player. That player remains with the object on the extended palm, so the operator can suspend the pendulum over it.

Now the question, spoken or silent, is "Does this item belong to this person?" The pendulum should, before too long, react according to its established code for answering *Yes* or *No* (See page 48). After it has settled down to one of these two movements, the person holding the item is asked if he/she is the owner.

If the pendulum's response is *No* and the person confirms this, the same item is tried on the next person, and so on. If it is *Yes* from both pendulum and person, the owner removes the item from the game but personally remains a participant. At this point, however, the pendulum operator takes another item from the box, places it upon the palm of the next person, and proceeds as before.

If the pendulum signals *No* when the true answer is *Yes*, this too puts the item out of the game—its ownership has had to be stated—and the owner remains as a participant; but the pendulum operator relinquishes office and hands over to the next in order of lot, who takes a fresh item from the box and continues. If the pendulum gives *Yes* when the true answer is *No*, then the ownership of the item remains unknown and it is tested upon another person's hand, but—as in the other case of error—the pendulum operator is changed. If a new operator chances to be the owner of the object then in circulation, he or she simply removes it from the game and take another item from the box.

Play continues until there are no more items left, or until every player has had a turn with the pendulum.

(Another version of this game follows, which is well worth using as people become more advanced; it calls for somewhat more preparation beforehand.)

Whose Name?

Each player writes his or her name, in the form which is most often used. All the written names are collected and are taken, with the covered box described in the previous game, to a helper who is not a member of the group and does not know most of the members.

All the names are then copied out (preferably typed) by this helper, on a sheet of paper which is afterwards cut into small slips, a name upon each. Each slip of paper is then enclosed in a "case" made of two little squares of card taped together on opposite sides, so the slips can easily be removed but can't easily fall out by accident. These encased slips are then put by the helper into the covered box. Each name can be used on two or three slips, and there can also be some blanks.

The game is then played in almost the same way as "Whose?" but the player on whose palm one of the encased slips is laid has, of course, no means of knowing whether the name inside is his/her own or not. The question asked by the operator, on suspending the pendulum over the case, is "Does this name belong to this person?" When the pendulum has responded, the player who is holding the slip takes it out and shows it to see if the response was correct. *(Blanks always count as "No.")* In any event, that slip is then removed from the game. A fresh item is then drawn from the box to be placed on the palm of the next player. As in "Whose?" the pendulum operator remains "in office" until his or her pendulum gives a wrong response; then the next operator in order of lot takes over.

The game continues until every player has had a turn as operator.

As the players have not seen or touched the slips bearing their names before the game, and each slip is withdrawn after being looked at, this game is a strict trial of the players' dowsing ability. It is not a "test," not being geared for each operator to use a standard number of slips, but it is an interesting challenge for those of some degree of proficiency, and is a proportionately good energizer.

In the above games, only the essentials are given; each group can decide the finer points for itself.

DOWSING RECORD

Name _____ Date _____

Instrument _____ Time start _____ end _____

Directive _____ Moon Phase _____ Sign _____

Object sought _____ Weather _____

Reason _____ Barometric Pressure _____

Area dowsed _____

Map used _____

Observations:

Results:

Notes for further work:

Checkpoint
7

- Dowsing is a natural faculty of the subrational levels of our being.

- In the dowsing process, the emotional-instinctual level of the psyche—
  - (a) acquires information from the astral world through its various modes of perception and questing, and
  - (b) utilizes astral substance to signal its findings to the outer world.

- The dowsing instrument is the indicator of the astral signalling force, and is also a focal point for the dowser's attention.

- The dowsing faculty becomes active when the

213

attention is completely absorbed; this is an "altered state of consciousness" although not generally recognized as such.

- *Remanence,* "the tendency of conditions to remain," is a cause of error generally known to dowsers, in which impressions of bygone material objects are picked up as if still present. Impressions of a future state of things are also likely to register occasionally as if presently existing.

- It is the astral counterpart of an object, whether past, present or future, which affects the dowsing instrument, not the material object itself.

- *Decide upon and make your first dowsing instrument!* (You can build up a collection, in time.)

- Try out the method of holding and using your dowsing instrument indoors if you wish, but take it outdoors, preferably into the open country, for real practice in its use.

- When you want to begin developing the faculty of dowsing, take time to sit down and talk aloud to your astral being, gently, kindly and with authority. Assure it of your love and appreciation: let it know why dowsing is necessary to your happiness, claim its help in mastering the art.

- Repeat this address to your astral being from time to time. The more you acknowledge and encourage your astral being, the more support and achievement it will bring to you.

- Keep up your good diet and simple life-style, keep up your contacts with the world of nature, the human world and the world within.

- Before setting out on a dowsing expedition, provide yourself with a *directive*, something to link you with your object of search.

- Using the directive and your dowsing instrument, *program yourself* for your dowsing expedition:
  (a) Familiarize yourself with the directive
  (b) Caress, warm and talk to your dowsing instrument. (It is the representative of your astral being.)

- If when making your first few dowsing expeditions you have the help of an experienced dowser, that's fine and you should make more rapid progress. You may however temporarily pick up some of that dowser's particular "idiom."

- When you go out dowsing by yourself, your dowsing instrument will develop a particular and individual code with you, and you will also discover what is your best object of search.

- You can't mistake a genuine dowsing signal: whether it is weak or strong, it feels like an invisible person trying to take control of the instrument. Have patience in establishing what different types of signal mean.

- If you group takes up dowsing, organize interesting and worthwhile expeditions to localities where there are specific things to dowse for. *But conversations can't be carried on while dowsing;* the social side must wait until afterwards.

- Don't let your group forget their Tabor Formulation when going on a dowsing expedition. The best time and place for it is likely to be on arriving at your destination.

- *Pendulum dowsing* is an art in itself. The pendulum has some disadvantages for outdoor work, but for indoor exploration and inquiry it is a wonderful instrument.

- Practice map-dowsing, and practice using a photograph as directive. Thus you'll come to realize the true astral level of this activity, and in an emergency (such as a search for a lost person) you may render real service.

- When programming yourself for a session of pendulum dowsing, don't forget to talk to your pendulum and bring it into the endeavor; it is a real dowsing instrument, and a representative of your astral being.

- Play astral power games for experience and insight into activities similar to dowsing. They are good as group activities—
    - (a) before taking up dowsing, as an introduction to some of the powers and forces involved.
    - (b) for the group while learning dowsing, as a welcome social activity, to keep up the united group spirit, and as an energizer.

- "Magnets" lets you feel what it's like to be a dowsing instrument. "Hot Trail" has you finding, without a dowsing instrument, which article in a room has been deliberately touched by the other members of the group. "Whose?" and "Whose name?" are pendulum games; the second one is a real trial of competence in dowsing, and is meant for the experienced.

The Llewellyn
TEST SHEET FOR USE WITH ESP CARDS

Sheet # _____

Date _____

Person
testing _____

Person
tested _____

Purpose of test _____

Comments:

No.	Card taken	Call	No.	Card taken	Call	No.	Card taken	Call
1			1			1		
2			2			2		
3			3			3		
4			4			4		
5			5			5		
6			6			6		
7			7			7		
8			8			8		
9			9			9		
10			10			10		
11			11			11		
12			12			12		
13			13			13		
14			14			14		
15			15			15		
16			16			16		
17			17			17		
18			18			18		
19			19			19		
20			20			20		
21			21			21		
22			22			22		
23			23			23		
24			24			24		
25			25			25		

Additional copies of this test sheet can be obtained in packages of 100 sheets for $3.00 plus $1.00 postage and handling. Order "Psychic Powers ESP test sheets" from Llewellyn Publications, P.O. Box 43383-DPP, St. Paul, MN 55164, U.S.A.

Appendix

A

ESP testing with the deck of twenty-five cards has developed certain accepted standards.

If you want the test results of your group to be considered by some particular organization, or if you want to work along with another group in any special line of research, you should find out exactly what their test conditions are, and/or let them know what yours are, so these can be coordinated. This can save a lot of wasted effort and disappointment.

Within your own group, certainly you can, and should, experiment and research to invent new methods of testing or to create new means of isolating the faculty it is intended to test. If you discover something good and original, there will surely be a place for it! The following notes however will help you make a start with your tests on generally acceptable lines.

The first thing you need is a screen behind which the operator can work with the cards. To have the operator in the next room with the door closed is, of course, just as good if not better. Have no mirrors anywhere in sight, even though you may feel it is impossible for any given mirror to reflect the cards at any stage of the proceedings.

If you use an actual screen, make sure it really prevents anyone seeing around the sides or over the top, and have the operator sitting at a table immediately behind and facing the screen.

A card-holder is also useful, especially for use in "card unseen" tests. A good simple type can be made from a double thickness of fairly thick cardboard, about fourteen inches tall and ten inches wide, having photo-frame fittings at the back so it can be made to stand almost vertically. The front thickness of board has a hole cut out, near the top, slightly larger each way than one of the cards, so when the two thicknesses of board are fixed closely together it makes a recess into which a card may be easily fitted. If you drill a pinhole in the back of the recess it will give you an easy means of pushing the card out again.

Now cut two lengths of narrow picture-frame strip, each as long as from the top of the recess to the foot of the board minus a fraction more than the height of a card. Tack or glue these strips onto the board parallel to each other, starting at the top of the recess, each undercut edge being along one edge of the recess.

When the holder is set up, the operator can place the ESP cards face downwards near by, take one and place it upright with its face against the board at the foot of the runway, then slide it up the runway and into the recess without danger of seeing its face at any moment. At the same time, the card is effectively segregated so there can be no confusion as to which card is the object of the test.

When cards are to be seen by the operator, they likewise can be singled out by placing them in the cardholder, but with the face displayed.

Also within the operator's easy reach there should be a bell or the control of an electric sound-signal, to be used when a new card has been put up. If the operator is in a separate room, it is very convenient to have an incoming signal also, so the operator can know when the person under test is ready for the next card. Ordinary bells can be used if they will be plainly audible.

In an "unseen" test (see Chapter 2), used cards as they are removed from the holder should be stacked, the latest on top, still face down. *When the series is over* the whole stack can be faced up, and the cards can be entered in order on the score sheet, in the column headed "Card taken". The person being tested, or a helper with that person, will have kept a list of the "calls" during the test—that is, of the guesses made—and this list will be entered in the "Calls" column. It can then be seen at a glance if each card called corresponds to the card taken and whether any pattern exists in the relationship of the columns.

A basic form of the score-sheet, which covers the essentials, is given in front of this Appendix.

There are a few other basic standards for the conduct of ESP tests, which, again, may be changed or added to by any testing body for its own use. The following is a good minimum.

1. From before the beginning until after the end of each test, or continuous series of tests, nobody is allowed to be behind the screen with the operator. Where the operator is in an adjoining room instead of behind a screen, nobody else is allowed to be in that room during tests.

2. No unnecessary conversation should be audible either to the operator or to the person being tested, and no avoidable sound except for the agreed signals. Of course, tests can be arranged purposely to explore the effect of different types of sound, rhythm or music on the accuracy of ESP.

3. There should be an agreed time limit for response. Most people under test will in any case prefer to reply on each card as soon as it is signalled, but there are some who will tend, at first, to make a delay. This is mostly due to nervousness, but is not helpful as it gives the conscious mind a chance to regain control in matters in which it is not competent. A photographic timer, set for sixty seconds, can be looked after by a helper, and placed within sight of the person being tested until

prompt reply is habitual.

You should also keep a log-book, in which all meetings and activities of your group, and other relevant matters, are to be entered. It takes a fair amount of experience to know where to draw the line between a full record and irrelevant chit-chat, but this experience is only gained through action. If you keep your log in simple note form, you can get quite a lot into it without too much effort.

You must include the date of the meeting, who is in charge (someone should be, in any circumstances) and who is present; how long the meeting lasts, what activities take place. Except for such tests as are covered by score-sheets, state results. If any plans or resolutions are made for future meetings, write these in too, and ensure anyone else who wants to enter the decision in their own log gets all the details. This can save time and trouble later.

In the front of your log-book you could list the names and dates of birth of all members, and remember to make entries later for newcomers. If you get any outstanding psychics, or "psychic twins," for instance, put in whatever may be relevant about them, including anything unusual about their health if they are willing to discuss it. Your group may also feel inclined to put in weather notes (including barometric readings), the phases of the moon, etc. Any details may be valuable in connection with some special research program; and there's no reason why you should not include more, or less, at some future date!

For testing with ESP cards, it has been established that a score of 5 responses correct out of 25 is "hazard level": that is, it is predictable that a person with no special development of psychic ability will achieve *as an average* (over a range of, say, ten runs of the 25 cards) a score of about 5 in 25, or in other words twenty per cent.

Single test results are not in themselves regarded very highly, although if a person has a rating of, say, 7% most of the time, and suddenly produces a score of 85%, any special circumstances are worth checking out if that is possible.

The 20% standard can equally be applied to any testing of a psychic ability, provided comparable test conditions can be used where there is only one correct answer out of five choices. In other cases, such as pendulum tests where all that is required is that the questions be answered with yes-or-no replies, chance, or hazard level, is 50%. (To make your "yes-no" scores compare with the standard 1 out of 5 system, multiply your yes-no percentage by .40). The questions themselves will not be entered on the score-sheet, only the number of the question. A basic form of the score-sheet for yes-no questions for the pendulum is given at the end of this Appendix.

The only other point which needs to be remarked here is that you are likely, occasionally, to find a person who consistently maintains an average score of less than "hazard level." Strangely enough, *this person is manifesting a psychic ability:* a consistent lower-than-hazard score could not occur unless some level of the psyche were either suppressing replies known to be true, or maybe reversing all replies. *It is not advisable to "dig" for the cause of this.* It should simply be recognized that the person is in fact manifesting "reversed effect" psychic ability, and that perhaps with recognition and practice the manifestation may adjust itself.

The Llewellyn
TEST SHEET FOR USE WITH YES-NO QUESTIONS

Sheet # _____

Date _____

Person
testing _____   Person
                                  tested _____

Purpose of test _____

Comments:

No.	True Reply	Reply Given	No.	True Reply	Reply Given	No.	True Reply	Reply Given
1			1			1		
2			2			2		
3			3			3		
4			4			4		
5			5			5		
6			6			6		
7			7			7		
8			8			8		
9			9			9		
10			10			10		
11			11			11		
12			12			12		
13			13			13		
14			14			14		
15			15			15		
16			16			16		
17			17			17		
18			18			18		
19			19			19		
20			20			20		
21			21			21		
22			22			22		
23			23			23		
24			24			24		
25			25			25		

Additional copies of this test sheet can be obtained in packages of 100 sheets for $3.00 plus $1.00 postage and handling. Order "Psychic Powers ESP test sheets" from Llewellyn Publications, P.O. Box 43383-DPP, St. Paul, MN 55164, U.S.A.

Appendix

B

The Tabor Formulation is to be used at the opening of meetings, as an immediate preparation for shared work. The energy thus mutually built up and circulated will create an atmosphere of enhanced understanding and fellowship, and, above all, will dynamically strengthen the psychic rapport of the group.

It is assumed that all members of the group have completely familiarized themselves, for their individual use, with the practice of the Tabor Formulation as given in Chapter 1. The practice given here is identical, excepting that this is done in group and requires a director who, while also participating in the meditation, has the task of cueing the others into its various stages.

As a preliminary, the group should decide on the

two mantrams to be used in Stage 3: these may be general in significance, or may relate specifically to the further activity of the occasion.

Practice

The participants are seated in a circle (no crossed legs or ankles) with hands linked as they will be throughout the Formulation, right palm downward, left palm upward.

1. The director announces the commencement of the meditation. The participants, with bowed heads and fixed gaze, turn their attention to their *Simple Breathing.* It is not necessary in this that the breathing should be in any way standardized; each person should find his or her own easy, natural rate and depth.

2. When the director feels it to be right, he announces entry into the second stage of the meditation. Each meditator now develops *Awareness of the Light,* attention being kept on that and on the breath.

3. When the director feels it to be right, he announces entry into the third stage and speaks, once, the two chosen mantrams. Each meditator now continually repeats in *Silent Utterance* the two mantrams, one on the in-breath and one on the out-breath, while retaining awareness of the light and of the breathing.

4. Finally, the director announces the close of the meditation practice, and the group proceeds to its further activities.

N.B. When the Tabor Formulation is first used in

in the group, several sessions should be devoted to it alone so that the members may be quite at ease with it before proceeding to other practices. Even after this the group will find it advantageous from time to time to devote a meeting to the Tabor Formulation alone, so as to polish it as an important key practice in psychic development, not regarding it merely as a preliminary. Such occasions will also provide opportunity to bring new members into group working.

LOG BOOK & DIARY

Group Name _____   Date of Session _____

Leader _____   Time start _____ end _____

Activities _____   Place _____

Weather _____   Moon Phase _____ Sign _____

Barometer Reading _____   Aspects _____

Other Conditions _____

Members Present:

Results Noted:

Date of next session _____ Time _____ Place _____

Plans for next session:

Glossary

ALTERED STATE OF CONSCIOUSNESS *A state in which a person is to some extent withdrawn from normal awareness of the material world. Some altered states are so slight as to be accepted without notice, others are easily recognized as one or another degree of* trance *(which see).*

ARCHETYPE *A universal and imageless concept; here, in the sense used by C. G. Jung, such a concept existing within the collective unconscious mind of humanity.*

ARCHETYPAL IMAGE *The Form in which an archetype is clothed by a particular culture, mythology, religion or individual.*

ASTRAL *Pertaining to that level of existence which is finer and more penetrating than matter but denser than mind. In* the psyche, it comprises the emotional/instinctual levels which unite mind and body.

AURA *An emanation of energy given out by, and forming a force-field surrounding, a living being.*

COUNTERPART *The astral level of an animate or inanimate material object. The counterpart can persist after the material object, as such, has ceased to exist.*

DIRECTIVE (sometimes, especially in pendulum dowsing, called a "Witness"). *A sample or representative of what is sought, used as an aid in dowsing.*

DISCARNATE *Without a physical body. Discarnate beings can have* become separated from their physical bodies (e.g., human souls after death) or may never have had earthly bodies (e.g., archangels, elementals.)

DIVINATION *Discovery of the future or of the unknown, usually by a specific technique rather than spontaneously.*

DOWSING *A method for seeking out material objects, and living beings, usually with the use of a "fork" or other instrument.*

ELECTRO-ENCEPHALO-GRAM *A chart, made by means of electric terminals attached to a person's head and connected to a tracing instrument, to show changes in electric potential in the brain.*

ELEMENTAL *A "nature-spirit", one of the living beings of the Astral World; less individuated than human beings, subrational, highly sensitive, emotional and imitative.*

ENTHUSIASM *A word of Greek origin, which initially meant "inspiration or possession by a god"; in our context, an emotional interest which can lead to total absorption of attention in a subject and hence to some degree of "altered state of consciousness" (which see).*

ESP *Generally-used abbreviation for "extra-sensory perception", that is, the gain of awareness without using the physical senses.* Pure ESP, *such a gain of awareness directly from the subject-matter, not taking it by telepathy*

from the mind of another.

HAZARD *"Pure chance."* In testing with a standard-plan deck of ESP cards, the average of right answers which can be expected from a "randomed" machine or a person of no psychic ability is termed "hazard level": in practice this is 20% (5 correct in 25). Both higher than hazard and lower than hazard averages are significant.

HYPNAGOGIC STATE A state between sleep and wakefulness, which can tend in either direction. In this state, the consciousness becomes intermittently invaded by images and impulses from the unconscious.

INSTINCT An innate, sub-rational and usually

unconscious impulse, prompting living beings to act in given ways in certain situations which are critical in their lives.

MANTRAM *A word, phrase or sentence repeated during devotion or meditation.*

MEDIUM *(in Spiritualism). A person who becomes an* intermediary *by providing the spirits with means of communicating with the incarnate.*

PROPHECY *A declaration of something which is in the future or otherwise ordinarily unknown. The word is often reserved to instances in which the seer obtains knowledge by contact with the Divine.*

PSYCHE *The non-material part of a psycho-*

physical being.

PSYCHOKINESIS, *see* Telekinesis.

PSYCHOMETRY *The faculty of gaining knowledge about an object, or about any matter associated with it, by handling the object.*

REMANENCE *(in Dowsing) Occurrence of reactions relating to a bygone material object or condition, as if the object or condition were still present.*

SCRYING *Divination by allowing the eyes to rest on a plain surface so that the mind becomes stilled, and receptive to imagery which arises from the Unconscious.*

SELF, Higher *That part*

of the psyche which is more elevated than the rational consciousness: *the spirit.* Lower Self, *the rational consciousness with the emotional/ instinctual nature and the physical body.*

SPIRIT *(1) The highest level of the psyche. (2) an elemental, or other being which is disembodied by nature. (3) In Spiritualism, a disembodied human soul.*

SUBLIMINAL *Literally "below the threshold"; here applied to experience or knowledge which enters the psyche, and can even result in action,* without itself coming to consciousness.

TELEKINESIS, *sometimes known as* Psychokinesis. *Movements caused in an object by psychic (that is, astral) means.*

TRANCE *An "altered state of consciousness", especially the more withdrawn degrees resembling sleep or sleepwalking.*

VISUALIZE *To form a mental image. The important factor for success in this is the knowledge that the image is to be mental, not an optical illusion. It can however seem to be optically visible.*

STAYING IN TOUCH

On the following pages you will find listed, with their current prices, some of the books now available on related subjects. Your book dealer stocks most of these, and will stock new titles in the Llewellyn Series as they become available.

However, to obtain our full catalog, and to keep informed of the new titles as they become available, you may write for our bi-monthly newspaper/catalog. A sample copy is free, and it will continue coming to you at no cost as long as you are an active mail customer. Or you may keep it coming for a full year with a donation of just $2.00 ($5.00 for Canada & Mexico, $10.00 overseas, first class mail).

Stay in touch! Included are news and reviews of new books, announcements of meetings and seminars all over the country, articles helpful to our readers, news of our authors, advertising of products and services, etc.

LLEWELLYN'S NEWS & REVIEWS
LLEWELLYN PUBLICATIONS, P.O. BOX 43383-DPP
St. Paul, MN 55164-0383, U.S.A.

TO ORDER BOOKS

If your book dealer does not have the books described on the following pages readily available, you may order them direct from the publisher by sending full price in U.S. currency, plus $1.00 each for postage and handling within the United States, $2.00 each for surface mail outside the United States, or $7.00 each for foreign Airmail.

FOR GROUP STUDY AND PURCHASE

Because there is a geat deal of interest in Group Discussion and Study of the subject matter of this book, we feel that we should encourage the adoption and use of this particular book by such groups by offering a special "quantity" price to Group Leaders or "Agents".

Our Special Quantity Discount, for a minimum order of five copies of THE LLEWELLYN PRACTICAL GUIDE TO THE DEVELOPMENT OF PSYCHIC POWERS is $22.00, Cash With Order. This price includes postage and handling within the United States. If Minnesota resident, then add the state sales tax. For additional quantities, please order in multiples of five. For Canadian and foreign orders, ease enquire. Credit Card (VISA, MasterCharge, American Express, Diners' Club) Orders are accepted. Charge Card orders may be phoned free by dialing 1-800-THE MOON. Mail orders to:

LLEWELLYN PUBLICATIONS
213 E. 4th St., P.O. Box 43383-DPP
St. Paul, MN 55164-0383, U.S.A.

THE LLEWELLYN PRACTICAL GUIDES
by Melita Denning & Osborne Phillips

THE LLEWELLYN PRACTICAL GUIDE TO ASTRAL PROJECTION.
Yes, your consciousness can be sent forth, out-of-the-body, with full awareness and return with full memory. You can travel through time and space, converse with non-physical entities, obtain knowledge by non-material means, and experience higher dimensions.

Is there life-after-death? Are we forever shackled by Time & Space? The ability to go forth by means of the Astral Body, or Body of Light, gives the personal assurance of consciousness (and life) beyond the limitations of the physical body. No other answer to these ageless questions is as meaningful as experienced reality.

The reader is led through the essential stages for the inner growth and development that will culminate in fully conscious projection and return. Not only are the requisite practices set forth in step-by-step procedures, augmented with photographs and "puts-you-in-the-picture" visualization aids, but the vital reasons for undertaking them are clearly explained. Beyond this, the great benefits from the various practices themselves are demonstrated in renewed physical and emotional health, mental discipline, spiritual attainment, and the development of "extra faculties".

Guidance is also given to the Astral World itself: what to expect, what can be done—including the ecstatic experience of Astral Sex between two people who project together into this higher world where true union is consumated free of the barriers of physical bodies.

0-87542-181-4, 239 pages, 5¼ x 8, softcover   **$6.95**

SUPPLEMENTAL DEEP MIND TAPE
THE LLEWELLYN DEEP MIND TAPE FOR ASTRAL PROJECTION.
This is a tool so powerful that it is offered only for use in conjunction with the above book. The authors of this book are adepts fully experienced in all levels of psychic development and training, and have designed this 90-minute cassette tape to guide the student through full relaxation and all the preparations for projection, and then—with the added dimension of the authors personally produced electronic synthesizer patterns of sound and music—they program the Deep Mind through the stages of awakening, and projection of, the astral Body of Light. And then the programming guides your safe return to normal consciousness with memory—enabling you to bridge the worlds of Body, Mind and Spirit.

The Deep Mind Tape is a powerful new technique combining guided Mind Programming with specially created sound and music to evoke deep level response in the psyche and its psychic centers for controlled development, and induction of the OUT-OF-BODY EXPERIENCE.

3-87542-201, 90-minute cassette tape.   **$9.95**

Note: If you have the book, THE LLEWELLYN PRACTICAL GUIDE TO ASTRAL PROJECTION, you may order this DEEP MIND TAPE by sending full price, plus $1.00 postge & handling ($7.00 overseas airmail). Or, you can order both Book AND Tape for a special price of just $15.00 Postpaid in U.S.A. ($25.00 overseas airmail).

THE LLEWELLYN PRACTICAL GUIDE TO PSYCHIC SELF-DEFENSE AND WELL-BEING. Psychic Well-Being and Psychic Self-Defense are two sides of the same coin—just as physical health and resistance to disease are:

> **FACT: Each person (and every living thing) is surrounded by an electro-magnetic Force Field, or AURA, that can provide the means to Psychic Self-Defense and to dynamic Well-Being.**

This book explores the world of very real "psychic warfare" that we all are victims of:

> **FACT: Every person in our modern world is subjected, constantly, to psychic stress and psychological bombardment: advertising and sales promotions that play upon primitive emotions, political and religious appeals that work on feelings of insecurity and guilt, noise, threats of violence and war, news of crime and disaster, etc.**

This book shows the nature of genuine psychic attacks—ranging from actual acts of black magic to bitter jealousy and hate—and the reality of psychic stress, the structure of the psyche and its inter-relationship with the physical body. It shows how each person must develop his weakened aura into a powerful defense-shield— thereby gaining both physical protection and energetic well-being that can extend to protection from physical violence, accidents...even ill-health.

> **FACT: This book can change your life! Your developed aura brings you strength, confidence, poise...the dynamics for success, and for communion with your Spiritual Source.**

This book gives exact instructions for the fortification of the aura, specific techniques for protection, and the Rite of the First Kathisma using the PSALMS to invoke Divine Blessing. Illustrated with "puts-you-into-the-picture" drawings, and includes powerful techniques not only for your personal use but for group use.

0-87542-190-3, 250 pages, 5¼ x 8, softcover.   **$6.95**

THE LLEWELLYN PRACTICAL GUIDE TO THE MAGICK OF SEX. There are dimensions to love, to sex, and to romance that you have never before known—here fully described and fully developed in step-by-step procedures that will bring magick—TRUE "MAGICK"— to your relationship.

> **Love has lost its way in the tangle of techniques and jargon which have accompanied the sexual revolution of the last two decades. There has been a revolution, but the end result has only increased the yearning for more complete union and lasting relationship attainable through inter-action between partners at the psychic and spiritual levels as well as the physical and emotional.**

This book gives you all the techniques that will enable you to thus accomplish "the marriage of two souls" which is the goal of Magickal Sex. Here are psycho-physical energizers and the Mystical Kiss; Erotic Massage and the Charging Breath; the use of Fantasy to awaken your Primal Powers, to restore and enliven Romance, and to attain the Pure Love and Joy known to the Troubadours of medieval times; Extended lovemaking, without exhaustion, without impatience; the Psychologically and Spiritually Liberated Couple and Total Pleasure—rapture soaring above rapture; Cosmic Awareness Intercourse, worshiping the Divine in each other; Sexual Mysticism and Spiritual Attainment; Rites of Sex Magick for Material Success and Abundance; the Eight-Day Ritual for the Conception of a Child, with all the Glory and Blessings of Divine Power.

> **LOVE CAN BE THE BRIDGE TO A NEW AGE! Lovers have always felt their love to be more than personal—now you can make part of your life the full glory potential in the relationship between Man and Woman, and between Man/Woman united and the Universe.**

0-87542-192-X, 275 pages, 5¼ x 8, illust., soft cover.   **$6.95**

THE LLEWELLYN PRACTICAL GUIDE TO CREATIVE VISUALIZATION.

All things you will ever want must have their start in your mind. The average person uses very little of the full creative power that is his, potentially. It's like the power locked in the atom—it's all there, but you have to learn to release it and apply it constructively.

IF YOU CAN SEE IT...in your Mind's Eye...you will have it! It's true: you can have whatever you want—but there are "laws" to Mental Creation that must be followed. The power of the mind is not limited to, nor limited by, the Material World—Creative Visualization enables Man to reach beyond, into the Invisible World of Astral and Spiritual Forces.

Some people apply this innate power without actually knowing what they are doing, and achieve great success and happiness; most people, however, use this same power, again unknowingly, INCORRECTLY, and experience bad luck, failure, or at best unfulfilled life.

This book changes that. Through an easy series of step-by-step, progressive exercises, your mind is applied to bring desire into realization! Wealth, Power, Success, Happiness...even Psychic Powers...even what we call Magickal Power and Spiritual Attainment ...all can be yours. You can easily develop this completely natural power, and correctly apply it, for your immediate and practical benefit. Illustrated with unique, "puts-you-into-the-picture" visualization aids.

0-87542-183-0, 255 pages, 5¼ x 8, softcover.   **$6.95**

THE LLEWELLYN PRACTICAL GUIDE TO THE MAGICK OF THE TAROT. *How to Read, And Shape, Your Future.*

"To gain understanding, *and control,* of Your Life."—Can anything be more important? To gain insight into the circumstances of your life—the inner causes, the karmic needs, the hidden factors at work—and then to have the power to change your life in order to fulfill your real desires and True Will: that's what the techniques taught in this book can do.

Discover the Shadows cast ahead by Coming Events.

Yes, this is possible, because it is your DEEP MIND—that part of your psyche, normally beyond your conscious awareness, which is in touch with the World Soul and with your own Higher (and Divine) Self—that perceives the *astral shadows* of coming events and can communicate them to you through the symbols and images of the ancient and mysterious Tarot Cards.

Your Deep Mind has the power to shape those astral shadows—images that are causal to material events—when you learn to communicate your own desires and goals using the Tarot's powerful symbol language and the meditative and/or ritual techniques taught in this book to energize and imprint new patterns in the Astral Light.

This book teaches you both how to read the Tarot Cards: seeing the likely outcome of the present trends and the hidden forces now at work shaping tomorrow's circumstances, and then—as never before presented to the public—how you can expand this same system to bring these causal forces under your conscious control.

The MAGICK of the Tarot mobilizes the powerful inner resources of psyche and soul (the source of all Magick, all seemingly miraculous powers) by means of meditation, ritual, drama, dance for the attainment of your goals, including your spiritual growth.

0-87542-198-9, 252 pages, 5¼ x 8, illust., softcover.   **$6.95**

THE LLEWELLYN MYSTERY RELIGION SERIES

VOUDOUN FIRE: THE LIVING REALITY OF MYSTICAL RELIGION.
by Melita Denning & Osborne Phillips, photography by Gloria Rudolph.
OBJECTIVE PROOF OF SPIRITUAL REALITY. Here are spectacular full color photographs of actual psychic phenomena filmed during Voodoo rituals in Haiti...giving objective proof of powers and forces normally invisible, and of the Power and the Glory that is part of all valid religious, and magical, experience.

"This is a book of revelation!

"In it, the objective reality of the Loa—Haitian Gods—and of the paranormal phenomena of mystical religion is demonstrated.

"The fact that this is demonstrated through a level of consciousness not ordinarily experienced confirms the ancient teachings that it is we—not the Gods—who must open the way. And when we do, the Gods respond.

"This book restores religious phenomena to us, and at the same time reveals the likelihood that anyone of European descent can be sure that at least some of his ancestors followed religions very similar to Voudoun. Thus we see that such a powerful mystical religion with the personal experience of paranormal phenomena is our rightful heritage!

"Indeed—all Gods are One God—and the intimate and direct contact between Man and divinity, the continued presence of invisible powers, and the revelation needed by modern man if we are to save ourselves from total alienation from the Natural World that is our proper home.

"Yes, these photographs require the recognition of other dimensions to reality. But we are living in an Age when we see that all men are—as seen from another dimension—One Man, and that all life is but One Life. The plurality of the Gods is likewise a matter of dimension, but it is from this dimension that we must reach up to make contact with Divinity. It is for us to make a channel for the Power to manifest. And of the Christian churches, it is the Catholic Power, that resembles Voudoun sufficiently so that many of the Haitian Gods, as well as those of Santeria and other Spiritist religions, can be seen as saints in a different dress.

"Fire has always been associated with the Gods, and in these photographs, we see why: we see the "astral light" as streamers of Cosmic Fire. Perhaps, too, we can gain an understanding of Fire as a "gift of the Gods", for it is contact with this Cosmic Fire that seems to bring about the paranormal phenomena, the "going invisible", for example, of the mystical religions.

"When we restore the paranormal to religions, and when we see the role of religious worship as the opening of channels between Man and Divinity, then we also see the joyous relationship between Man and Nature, Man and man, and Man and the Spiritual Worlds. And we learn that all religions are One Religion, and in this we also find the necessity for the many ways through which men reach the Gods and relate to Divine Power."

(from the Introduction, by
Carl Llewellyn Weschcke, Publisher)

In this book, you see for yourself the ASTRAL FIRE that accompanies genuine ritual; you see the living presence of the LOA (the Haitian God-forces) as they are invoked; you witness the visible possession of the devotee by a spiritual entity, and the ecstasy upon her face. The text gives a concise history of Voudoun, tracing not only its African but Amerindian origins and its beginnings back into ancient Egypt. Parallels with Christianity and with pre-Christian European religions are demonstrated, and the distorted myths which represent Voodoo as evil are shown for what they are. The religion itself is analyzed, its dances, chants, musical and magical instruments, its gods and rituals described. Voudoun is made to come alive for the reader and its music is presented in words and score set to disco beat for personal experience.

0-87542-186-5, 182 pages 8½ x 11, 39 full page color plates, and nearly 100 black and white photographs and drawings, softbound. **$9.95**

THE MAGICAL PHILOSOPHY
by Melita Denning & Osborne Phillips

Here, in five hard-bound volumes, is a complete presentation of the Inner-Tradition of the Western World. Here the reader will find explained the basic structure of the Universe as we know it, and the basic structure of the Human Psyche; here, too, is the panorama of the Mind's search for understanding, and the Soul's ways of relating person and community to the tides of season and life; the foundations of the system of Magick by which Man trains and develops his inner faculties and consciously asserts his creative potential in all his life work; and the actual exercises, rituals and practices of a complete program of Magickal Work and Study developed by a Magickal Order founded in 1897.

Here, High Magick is seen as the power of the deep traditional wisdom activated by the lightning-flash of inspiration of the present moment: as the precious jewel of timeless experience transmuted to living, pulsing dynamism by the free spontaneous spirit of the Magician.

THE MAGICAL PHILOSOPHY is the only work in existence to reveal the inner system of symbolism, philosophy and spiritual technology which is at the heart of the mainstream occult tradition. In this work are keys that will unlock High Magick's innermost sanctuaries of magical power and understanding, presented in a structured and progressive curriculum of attainment which follows the intrinsic pattern of the psyche itself.

The work of Magick is the work of Man. The famous schema of the Qabalah, the "Tree of Life," which indicates an entire philosophy by means of ten circles and twenty-two connecting lines, is sometimes taken to be an objective plan of the universe. It is not: it is altogether subjective. It is the plan of the universe interpreted through the focusing lens of human nature. This is both the limit of what we can know and the limit of what concerns us. The perfection to which we aspire must be perfection of the human kind.

This aspiration towards perfection is essential to all who follow the path of Magick. Here is no place for scruples about spiritual narcissism, or pride, or anything of that sort. To reject this aspiration would be at least as great a catastrophe as the defects which it might seem to avoid. It is this aspiration, and the reverent sense of purpose which are the most sure marks of the true student of the Qabalah.

There is Man, the Microcosm, containing within himself all those forces he perceives in the external universe, and step by step, in his training, becoming aware of those forces and learning at the same time to evoke and control them, for this is the truth, which the guardians of the Qabalah have known through the ages, and which the most advanced psychologists are beginning to perceive: the inner world and the outer are more closely related than is ever dreamed by the average man, who thinks of himself as a victim of external circumstances; and the inner world is the more potent. Man makes his world, or is crushed by the worlds made by others. The greater his understanding and the more enlightened his spirit, the better he will carry out this essential task.

Man must be realized: he must be given awareness of the splendours which he can know, the attainment which should be his, the sublime bliss which is his true nature, the beauty and majesty of the universe in which he participates. This is the goal of this Work.

ROBE AND RING
BOOK I OF THE MAGICAL PHILOSOPHY

Most men worship divinity as God absolute or as one of many gods and pray to such divinity for goodness in life. For a small number this is not sufficient, and they seek instead a closer bond—to love or be loved by their God: these are the mystics. Of these, a smaller number exists for whom even this divine love is not enough. For these, the magicians, to know and love their God, it is necessary that they should realize and bring into their consciousness their own divinity.

This is the Western Magical Tradition. Its methods are active rather than passive, and ceremonial rather than meditative—although meditation is utilized when occasion requires. The secret of its initiatory teaching is that it should follow the lines of development of the psyche itself. It is western, too, in its emphasis upon the cultivation of the individual personality, and upon the attainment of conscious union and integration between the higher self and the ordinary personality.

In this book, you will discover the glory of the Western Tradition, here are the ethics, the ideals and aspirations of the Initiate, the vivid imagery, the rich ceremonial, the wonder and the wisdom of High Magick. In this book, you will understand the importance of FINDING YOUR TRUE WILL and following it to YOUR SELF-REALIZATION; you will learn how to begin "growing" your Magical Personality, and how to furnish your own personal Chamber of the Art.

0-87542-176-8, 192 pgs., 6 x 9, illust., hardbound. $10.00

THE APPAREL OF HIGH MAGICK
BOOK II OF THE MAGICAL PHILOSOPHY

The power of ritual to make contact with the hidden levels of the mind is very subtle, and yet very simple. No matter how deeply the subconscious mind may be buried beneath inhibitions, rationalizations or, frequently, beneath loads of ephemeral rubbish, one line of communication must remain open: that is through the sympathetic nervous system upon which we all depend to look after our digestion and our breathing, and even to keep ur heart beating while we sleep!

This book shows you the who and why of many forms of traditional symbolism, the "apparel" in which the Magician clothes his inner purposes so as to make an IRRESISTIBLE RITE for their fulfillment in the material world. It is with such symbolism that we catch the attention of more than the rational mind, reaching all levels of consciousness and welding them into a single instrument of power.

In this one book you will find the symbolism of minerals, gems and amulets; occult significance of metals, use of talismans, stones and colors; symbolism of the calendar; magical seasons of the year; mathematical views of the universe; plants and their occult significance; animal archetypes; the primary correspondences of ceremonial magick and the Qabalah; magical equipment and exoteric symbolism of the elemental weapons; the Tarot; the holy and mysterious Mansions of the Moon; Exercises, and techniques of Meditation.

0-87542-177-6, 176 pgs., 6 x 9, illust., hardbound. $10.00

THE SWORD AND THE SERPENT
BOOK III OF THE MAGICAL PHILOSOPHY
THE MAGICK OF YOUR CHOICE. Yes, you can build an original and workable system of Ceremonial Magick, based on the authentic traditions of the Qabalah and the Ritual Keys for activation and control of the ASTRAL LIGHT. Contrary to the ideas which have been put forward by traditional schools, Qabalah is a self-contained system needing neither Hebrew nor Christian dogma. Qabalah supplies the framework for any deific system—making POWER MAGICK THAT EXPRESSES YOUR WILL in perfect reciprocity with the Forces of the Cosmos.

> **You may not wish to use the traditional Hebrew forms, nor even the Greek or Roman forms whose correspondences on the Tree of Life have long since been established. YOU CAN EMPLOY WHATEVER MAY BE THE PANTHEON OF YOUR CHOICE—Celtic, AmerIndian, Haitian or other —and, by following the method set forth in this book, you can construct a valid system whose Qabalistic basis is firm.**

In this book you will learn the basic Qabalistic doctrines and the full range of correspondences—the mystical keys to consciousness. You will learn how the channels can be contacted by the appropriate rites, how the astral substance is molded by thought, etheric forces and Movement within the light, the Cosmic Tides, developmental exercises and magical techniques, and you will gain understanding of the nature of life and the world as we experience it. You will find instruction and guidance to the technique of Path-working, the use of incenses, the establishment of the Circle, the uses of Meditation.
0-87542-178-4, 265 pgs., 6 x 9, illust., hardbound. $10.00

THE TRIUMPH OF LIGHT
BOOK IV OF THE MAGICAL PHILOSOPHY
THE WISDOM OF THE WEST: the Western Mystery Tradition of self-development leading to that "descent of Light" crowning Man as KING—fulfilling human destiny—is based entirely on knowledge of the structure of the psyche. It is this that uniquely distinguishes the Western Way from the Eastern, and the modern from the old.

> **What is the true function of the Ego? How real is the psychic difference between Man and Woman? Can human love really "inspire" us? What is the reality of your "Holy Guardian Angel"? What is the Abyss? There is no "side-stepping" as these questions are answered, nor in the account of many other pertinent topics which are evaded by other authorities writing in this field.**

Here, in this book, is a luminous summing-up of Western Man's adventures in self-discovery; here is a guide-book in the relationship between psychological integration and occult progress; here is the deepest and yet most lucid exposition ever made of what actually takes place in the psyche at various stages of its progress. And, because this book embodies the principles of GNOSIS, to understand these matters IS TO UNDERGO INITIATION and to develop THE FOUNDATIONS OF PERSONAL POWER. Here are actual exercises for the opening of the Psychic Power Centers; here is a modern psychological understanding of established occult and magical concepts; and here is understanding of the life of the soul in terms meaningful in today's world.
0-87542-179-2, 251 pgs. 6 x 9, illust., hardbound. $10.00

MYSTERIA MAGICA
BOOK V OF THE MAGICAL PHILOSOPHY
THE INNER SECRETS REVEALED: The Secret Symbolism of the
Aurum Solis is given to you for the first time! The Gates to Knowledge.
Ecstasy. and Power are opened to give modern man powers
undreamed of in past ages. For those who would know the Meaning
of their lives. who do know that we are more than simple machines.
who believe—and would experience—there is Beauty and Love in
the Universe.

**No matter what your level of ability in Ceremonial Magick,
this is one of the most important books you could ever
own. Bringing together the best of the magical systems
of Egypt, Ireland, Pre-Columbian America, the Mediter-
ranean, Northern Europe and the Middle East, the authors
lead us into new and profound areas of Magical Work.
KNOWLEDGE IS POWER, AND THE KNOWLEDGE PRE-
SENTED IN THESE PAGES IS SOME OF THE MOST
POWERFUL EVER PUBLISHED.**

"...Whatever forms exoteric religion may have taken. the Western
approach to life has always been active and practical. There is. as
we recognize. a great body of magical knowledge. which as a means
of attainment is worthy to take its place among the great mystical
systems of the world; its neglect hitherto by so many serious
scholars. must be attributed to its wide scope and the multiplicity of
its levels. as well as to the atmosphere of secrecy with which in
many lands and ages it has been surrounded."

**MYSTERIA MAGICA offers you essential and profound
magical knowledge, authentic texts and formulae of the
Western Mystery Tradition which have hitherto been
hidden in inaccessible libraries, in enigmatic writings, or
in rarely-imparted teachings passed on only by word of
mouth; and, in addition, it contains ample sections
showing you how to use all that is disclosed, how to give
potent consecration to your own magical weapons, how
to build rites on the physical and astral planes with word
and action, sound, color and visualization, to implement
your own magical will.**

Here are secrets which have been guarded through centuries by an
elite among popes and rabbis. adepts and seers. dervishes and
mages. Here. explicitly set forth. is knowledge by which the mystical
priesthood of Egypt wielded true God-force through millennia and
which has aided and will aid devotee and thaumaturgist in establishing
bonds of knowledge. love and power with their chosen deific force
however named:

**The Setting of the Wards of Power (Greek and Hebrew
forms); The Setting of the Wards of Adamant (Sub Rosa
Nigra); the Clavis Rei Primae and Orante Formulae;
Banishing and Invoking; Identifying with God-forces;
Rising on the Planes; Astral Projection; Works under-
taken through Astral Projection; Formula of the Watcher;
Elementary techniques of Scrying; the Constellation of
the Worshipped; Principles of Ceremonial; the Dance as
Instrument of Magick; Images; Sigils, conjurations of the
Art; Enochian Studies (Text and Commentaries); Con-
secrations and the Use of the Magical Weapons; Sphere-
Working; Evocation to Visible Appearance; Transubstantion;
Consecration of a Talisman; and much more—with tables,
guidance to pronunciation of Enochian, workings with
Elementals, formulae for integration, etc.**

0-87542-180-6, 466 pgs., 6 x 9, illust., hardbound. $20.00

The above volumes may be purchased individually by sending full price plus $1 00 each
($7.00 each overseas airmail) for postage & handling. or may be purchased as a set of all five
volumes for $60.00 postpaid in U.S.A. ($75.00 total overseas airmail) Add 6% state sales tax
if Minnesota resident.